Young Woman

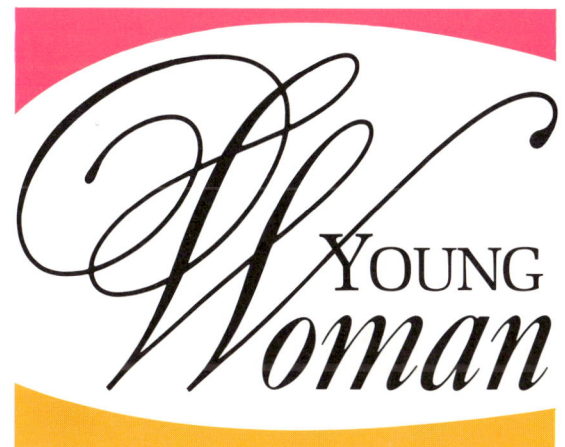

A Christian girl's guide to teenage sexuality

All Bible quotations are taken from the *Good News Bible* unless otherwise indicated.

Scriptures quoted from the *Good News Bible* published by The Bible Societies/HarperCollins Publishers Ltd., UK, © American Bible Society, 1966, 1971, 1976, 1992.

Scriptures quoted from the Holy Bible *New International Version* published by Hodder and Stoughton Ltd, UK, © New York International Bible Society.

ISBN 1-873796-63-3

Copyright © 1996
Autumn House Publishing
All rights reserved.
No part of this publication may be reproduced in any form without prior permission from the publisher.

Printed in England for
Autumn House Publications
Grantham, England

2nd printing 1996

Young Woman

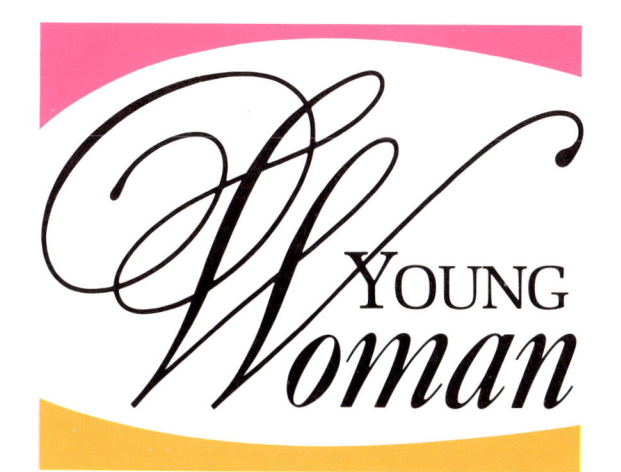

Jonathan and Ana Gallagher
have considerable experience in teenage, family and marriage counselling. They live in Hertfordshire, England, with their two teenage children.

Jonathan Gallagher has degrees in both the sciences and theology. He has a PhD from the University of St Andrews, Scotland. He is widely known for his stimulating seminars and lectures on Sexuality in Teenage Years, and enjoys working with young people.

Editor
DAVID MARSHALL
BA, PhD.

Medical Editor
EILEEN BAILDAM
MB, ChB, DCH, MRCGP, MRCP.

A Christian girl's guide to teenage sexuality

WHY WE WROTE IT

They said to us: 'Tell it straight, keep it short.'
Most of all they said, 'Make it relevant.'
'Because' — they said again — 'too much of this stuff is just so out of touch with today's reality.'

So, hoping that this is not *too* real for some, this book is for you. Not too 'airy-fairy romantic novel' but not too 'you do sex this way' either.

What we hope you're looking for is a Christian approach to the subject of sex. Not a step-by-step manual, nor some vague theories, but an honest and direct look at sexuality from a Christian perspective. Having counselled many over the years, we wanted to approach the subject from a practical standpoint using questions and answers *actually asked and replied to* from seminars on relationships, especially when working in Family Life ministries.

We would like to thank a variety of people for their interest in and contributions to this book. A number of young people have contributed their ideas, suggestions and questions. Others have kindly read through the book and given us their comments. But for the sake of confidentiality, we'll keep our thanks personal!

JONATHAN AND ANA GALLAGHER

Young Woman

CONTENTS

1   PAGE 8

Sex?

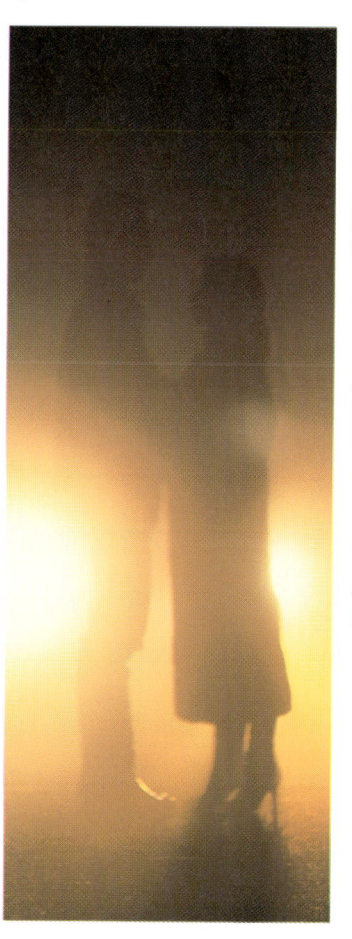

2   PAGE 20

What kind of person am I?

3   PAGE 37

What about me, physically?

4   PAGE 52

This crazy little thing called love

Young Woman

6   PAGE 79

God and sex

5   PAGE 64

Sex and the modern world

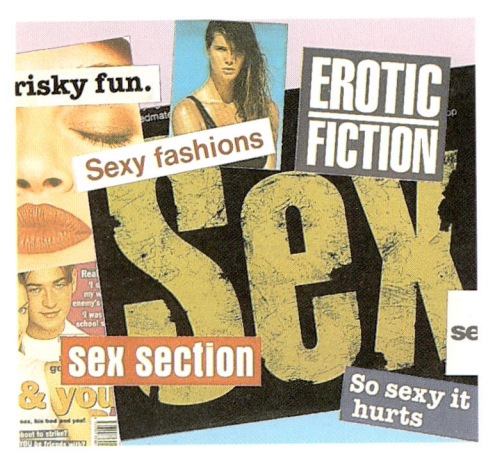

7   PAGE 94

Putting it into practice

8 PAGE 111

Problems and solutions!

9 PAGE 126

Broken sex

10 PAGE 142

WARNING! sex can seriously damage your health

11 PAGE 157

Sexual healing and the God of love

12 PAGE 172

The promise

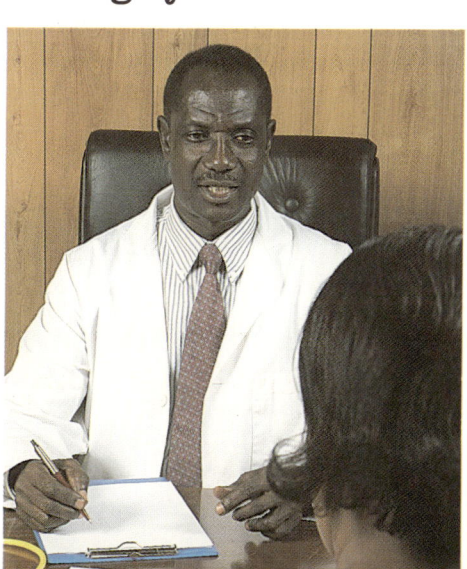

1

Sex?

In these last days some people will appear whose lives are controlled by their own lusts. 2 Peter 3:3.

QUESTIONS NEED ANSWERS

Sometimes it's easier to talk around a subject. Especially when you know some people will be offended, or embarrassed, or upset. But the only reason for writing this book is to speak very directly about sexuality, and how that fits into life and love. So if you are going to be offended, embarrassed, upset or all three then you might want to think again. For though we want to speak gently and sympathetically, we also want to be direct.

Why?

▶ Because questions, important questions, need answering. Questions girls like you are asking. And you deserve some honest answers from a Christian angle.

▶ Because otherwise others will tell you what is right and wrong, what you should do and what you shouldn't. Plenty of people would *love* to shape your understanding of sexuality — and some don't have your best interests at heart.

▶ Because you can't talk about sex by referring to butterflies or rabbits. You *have* to explain about how it really happens. We want to make it beautiful — as God made us all! Some people think sex is dirty and so they believe it's not something to talk about. What we want you to see is how wonderful it can be at the right time and in the right place.

DIFFERENT VIEWS ABOUT SEX

But how is sex spoken about where you are? Not at all, maybe. Or only in whispers, with lots of things not making much sense. Or in crude jokes.

Or is sex so common and usual, even between single people, that it's just like eating or breathing — something that has to happen and you just do it? A careless and casual approach to sex is as bad as treating it as dirty.

You really have to search hard to find a happy and a healthy view of sex. And it might surprise you to know that God has just such a view! We'll talk more about that later on. But for the moment we want you to look again at the way sex is treated where you are.

How is sex discussed?

How is sex treated on TV or on video or in the movies?

What do other people where you live think about sex?

How does your family view sex?

What influences your thinking about sex?

Where do you get your ideas about sex?

Isn't it true that sex is worrying enough without all the other pressures? You hardly have time to grow up before everybody's trying to tell you something — about how to behave, how to live, and how to think about sex.

WHAT 'ADVICE' ARE YOU GETTING?

Advice about sex comes from many sources. You need to think about where your ideas come from. Who's telling you what.

Look at some of what is being said, out there. We went out and took a look at some magazines especially for teenage girls. (Now in some places this may be different. But it seems that these magazines are giving their answers to the questions girls want to know. So what were their answers — especially about sexual issues?)

In answer to someone who wrote

Teenage girl magazines give a popular but distorted view of sex.

asking about premarital sex, one magazine printed this:

'I think it's a good idea to experiment sexually before marriage. That way you know if you're compatible.'

Already there's something to think about — and disagree with!

'A guide to loving' presented just pictures and descriptions of different sexual positions, and was clearly aimed at boy-friends and girl-friends, not married couples. Sex before marriage was seen as entirely normal, and to be encouraged with suggestions about how to do it. Another article in a teen magazine had the headline: 'How to become a better lover'. Again the reader was told how to improve his/her sexual performance — as if that was all that mattered.

One even gave step-by-step details on 'How to seduce your boy-friend.' Blatantly to offer advice and tips on how to be sexy and get your boyfriend into bed shows just how low the expectations of what is acceptable behaviour have sunk.

Of course, none of these articles spoke about the pain of premarital sex: the uncertainty, the guilt, the damage to you as a real person. Quite the opposite — one response to a letter from a girl saying she always felt guilty after having sex was, 'Don't feel guilty — just enjoy it.'

Such guidance to young people is really irresponsible. If you *are* going to discuss sex before marriage, you *must* talk about the pain and the problems too. It's not fair to anyone to make it all seem a bed of roses.

And often the talk about sex was not beautiful and caring, but crude and harsh. Topics like 'How to handle a hard-on' (a boy's erection). 'Wicked sex' was the title for an article on some odd sexual ideas that certainly are not good and right, and yet were suggested to teenagers. What was once seen as vice is now shown as normal.

IS SEX NORMAL BEFORE YOU'RE MARRIED?

That's what hit us hardest after reading these magazines. The message was that you're *supposed* to have sex with your boy-friend, and if you don't then you're weird or repressed or a failure.

Not just the magazines, either. On TV and in movies, sex is often set out as a natural requirement for being someone's girl-friend. No matter where you are in the world, the great themes are adultery, infidelity, betrayal, premarital sex, and all kinds of sexual exploitation — whether it's some soap opera or the latest movie blockbuster or romantic story book.

Take a quick glance at what's being offered in your area as entertainment. Looking carefully will reveal the usual catalogue of sexual sins, shown in all their 'glory' as normal behaviour between men and women.

That's one problem. Another is that there's still a lot of nonsense talked about sex — or it's not talked about at all. Wrong ideas about sex often come because people don't feel able to talk about such matters openly and honestly.

SEX: THE UNSPOKEN SUBJECT

In some places sex still is a taboo (forbidden) subject, and this is particularly true in some Christian societies. Historically, sex and Christianity have rarely been seen to be compatible!

In one survey of Christian young people, a large majority said they weren't satisfied with their Church's openness about giving advice on sexual matters. They weren't saying the sexual standards were wrong, they just wanted to know *what* was the Church's position and *why*.

Some religious people still believe that this is one subject that should *not* be talked about. They think this is a private matter between husbands and wives, and shouldn't be discussed in public.

The problem is that if Christian principles of sexuality are not made public, or not even talked about, then who wins? The other side, of course! So it's really important to explain, in an open and honest way, exactly what *are* the basic principles of virtue and morality.

WHAT HAPPENS IF YOU DON'T TALK ABOUT SEX?

What's the alternative? Well, if you ignore or deny or reject the need for Christian education about sex, then you will pay a heavy price. There will be more Christian teenage illegitimate pregnancies than the average (because they do not expect to have sex, or are ignorant about it). There will be more agony over specific needs for abortion (how can it be termed 'contraception'?). There will be more Christians affected by sexually-transmitted diseases contracted in innocence or foolishness . . . .

The truth is that many sexual disasters could be prevented through a better understanding of sexual behaviour, morality and most of all how this relates to our spiritual

For too many Christians discussions about sex are not for the teenager, only for parents — in private!

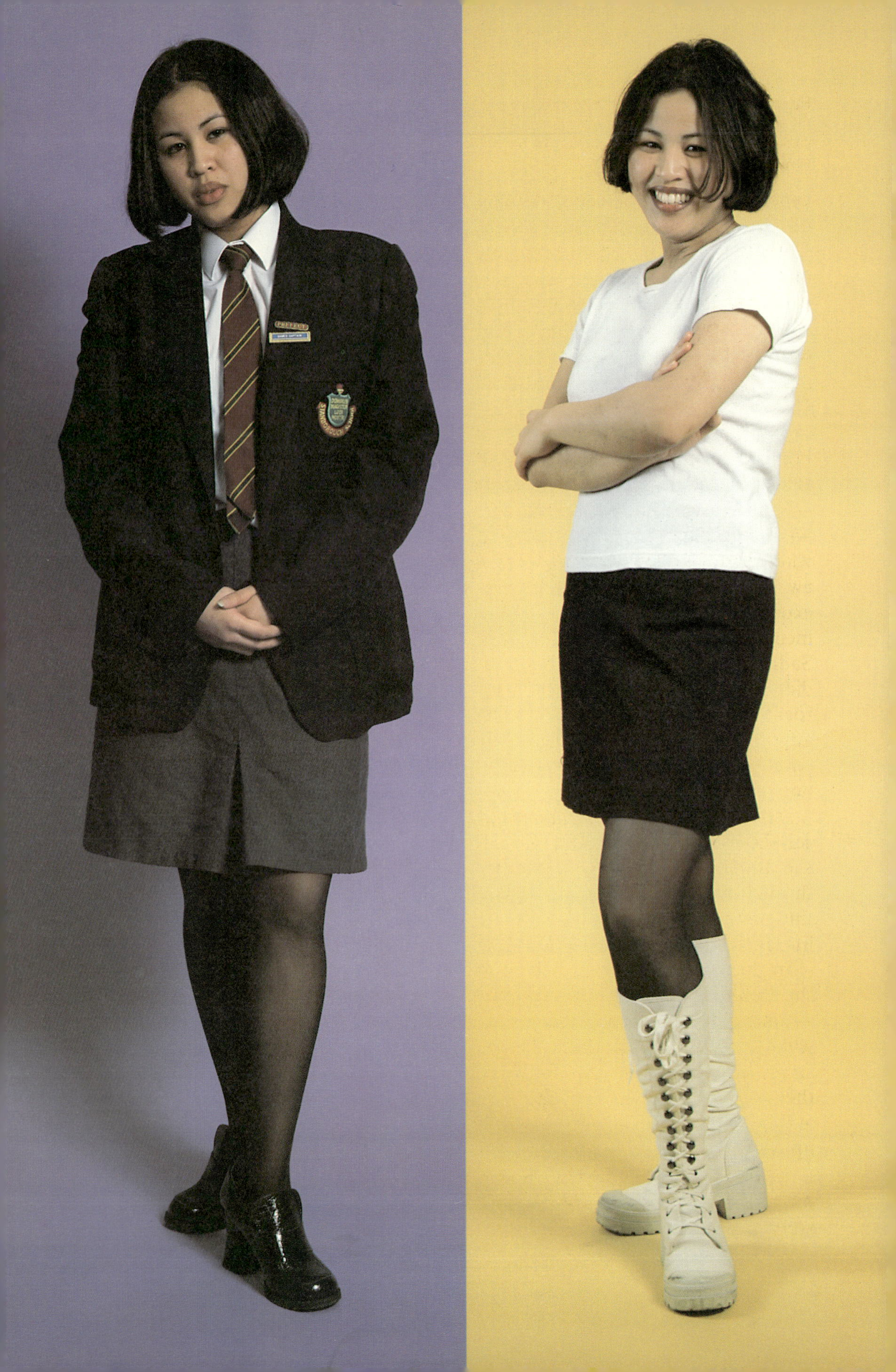

For many girls the transition from schoolgirl to the excitement of being a teenager can bring confusion about how to handle the arrival of sexual awareness.

experience. For the greatest damage of broken sex in the life of the Christian is what happens to God and us. Our relationship with God is wounded by guilt and shame, and we may even feel that we have destroyed God's plan for our lives.

JOY

Joy came from a happy Christian home. She had a good childhood. But when the time for changes came — puberty and all those hormones — her life became different from what she'd known before. Sexual awakening was fast and furious. She experimented with this new excitement as she began her teenage years. Sadly Joy either didn't know (or didn't want to know) about the need for control and caution. Ignoring advice, she rushed into a rollercoaster ride of sexual experiences in her search for fun.

Before Joy was of a legal age for sex she was dead. After trying what she thought was being grown up through all kinds of sex, she didn't find any meaning or purpose for her life. In the end she gave up looking.

In her note she indicated that she'd tried it all — especially the sex — and didn't find anything worthwhile. The last boy had been the last straw, and when that had finished, then she gave up looking for love and happiness through sex. She gave up on life.

And while that may be extreme, a number of girls have told us of their regrets. Sex doesn't solve the basic questions of life. On its own sex can't give meaning and purpose, whatever the advertisements say.

You need to learn fast, but not through playing with fire! Life is an exploration, but you don't have to repeat every last experiment. And when it comes to sex, make sure you don't leave God out of your thoughts.

Using sex as a source of entertainment and fun, as advertised by the media, can bring unadvertised grief.

QUESTIONS AND ANSWERS

Why is so much talked about sex?

Many reasons. 1. We live in a world that has dedicated itself to pleasure. This is the way most people wish to live: 'My enjoyment is number one.' 2. More and more, people have given up on God and religion, and so sex is a kind of substitute religion. 3. Old ideas of morals have been rejected, and so people believe they can do whatever they want. So premarital sex, adultery, divorce, sexual perversions and abuse become more common.
4. Sex is seen as fun and excitement. The media encourage this view, and so 'fun with sex' is made to be *the* most important thing in life.
5. Because if you don't talk about sex, then you're odd. And so on. The modern fascination with sex is all too often about selfishness.

What's wrong in finding out about sex for myself?

You do need to discover the truth about sex for yourself. But that doesn't mean doing it. With all the risks, you need to be very careful as you explore. You don't need to abuse drugs to see that this would be a problem. You don't have to throw yourself off a mountain to find out what it's like to fall to the bottom. And sex can be just as dangerous — especially with diseases like AIDS, as well as what can happen to your spirituality and self-worth. Be sensible. Take a look at the hard evidence. And then choose for yourself — not following the crowd, but doing what is good for yourself and others.

I can't find anyone I trust to talk about sexual feelings. What should I do?

It's not absolutely essential to talk to someone else, though this can help. Have you thought of discussing your thoughts with a church pastor (especially a youth pastor) or perhaps writing to someone who specializes in Christian counselling? But if there really is no one, then read plenty of good books (like this one, we hope!) and know what it's all about. And even if you can't talk directly to your family about these matters, you can still discuss marriage and family and children and so on.

Is sex that important?

Not to some people. And it's also true that to be completely absorbed by sex is no way to live either. Sex as a way of life is overrated.

But it *is* important to most people. Why? Because it is still the way we give ourselves most completely. We really show how much we love by making love. If sex doesn't bother you at the moment, then don't worry. You may still be developing, and other interests occupy you. But you still need to be aware of the rights and wrongs of sex — and be prepared for some surprises later on!

Clothes and behaviour have an irresistible appeal to any young male.

If all my friends are having sex, what's wrong with me trying it?

Do you always do what everybody else does? Are you just a sheep that follows blindly along? Don't you *want* to make decisions for yourself? Just because everybody does something, that doesn't make it right or good. The majority is not always right!

And how will you feel later, thinking, 'I only did this because everybody else did it'? What does that say about you as a person? And what does it say about love and specialness? Sex is too important to waste.

Wouldn't it be best to wait until I get married to find out about sex?

Yes, if you mean the actual physical side of sex. But you need to know some of the theory now, otherwise you might be fooled. You need to know how your body works, how sexual activity progresses, and how to stop!

You also need to know about both the beauty and the dangers of sex, so you can make it the best experience it can possibly be.

Why do girls and boys think so differently about sex?

Someone once said that girls use sex to get love, and boys use love to get sex. That's very cynical, but it does make some sense. Girls want the whole relationship — not just the physical. They want comfort and security, happiness and friendship. Boys are more physically direct, and can be sexually aroused more quickly. They can more easily see sex as being apart from love — or so it might seem. And the world has emphasized these differences. But the differences are not so great. Part of a loving relationship is to bring a boy and girl closer in their thoughts too. That's why it's so important to understand each other: mentally, physically and spiritually.

How can I avoid getting tempted?

A good question. Someone said the easiest way to end temptation is to give in to it. But that can never be a moral and Christian answer. To give in (especially to sexual temptation) is to say we are controlled by our desires. They are our masters, we are the servants. No one can have self-respect if they act like that.

Avoiding is the important word. Don't get into a situation that is obviously going to lead to temptation (like spending much time alone together in the dark). Don't encourage others either — to have excited your boy-friend by your clothes or behaviour and then feel tempted yourself is really dangerous.

Instead, plan activities together with others. Work together, spend time with each other's families, concentrate on doing things apart from the physical side of love.

Temptation may come (and there's nothing wrong in being tempted, remember. Even Jesus was tempted). You need to redirect your mind, and think on the good and positive.

Try sport together or some activity that you can enjoy that doesn't lead to compromising situations.

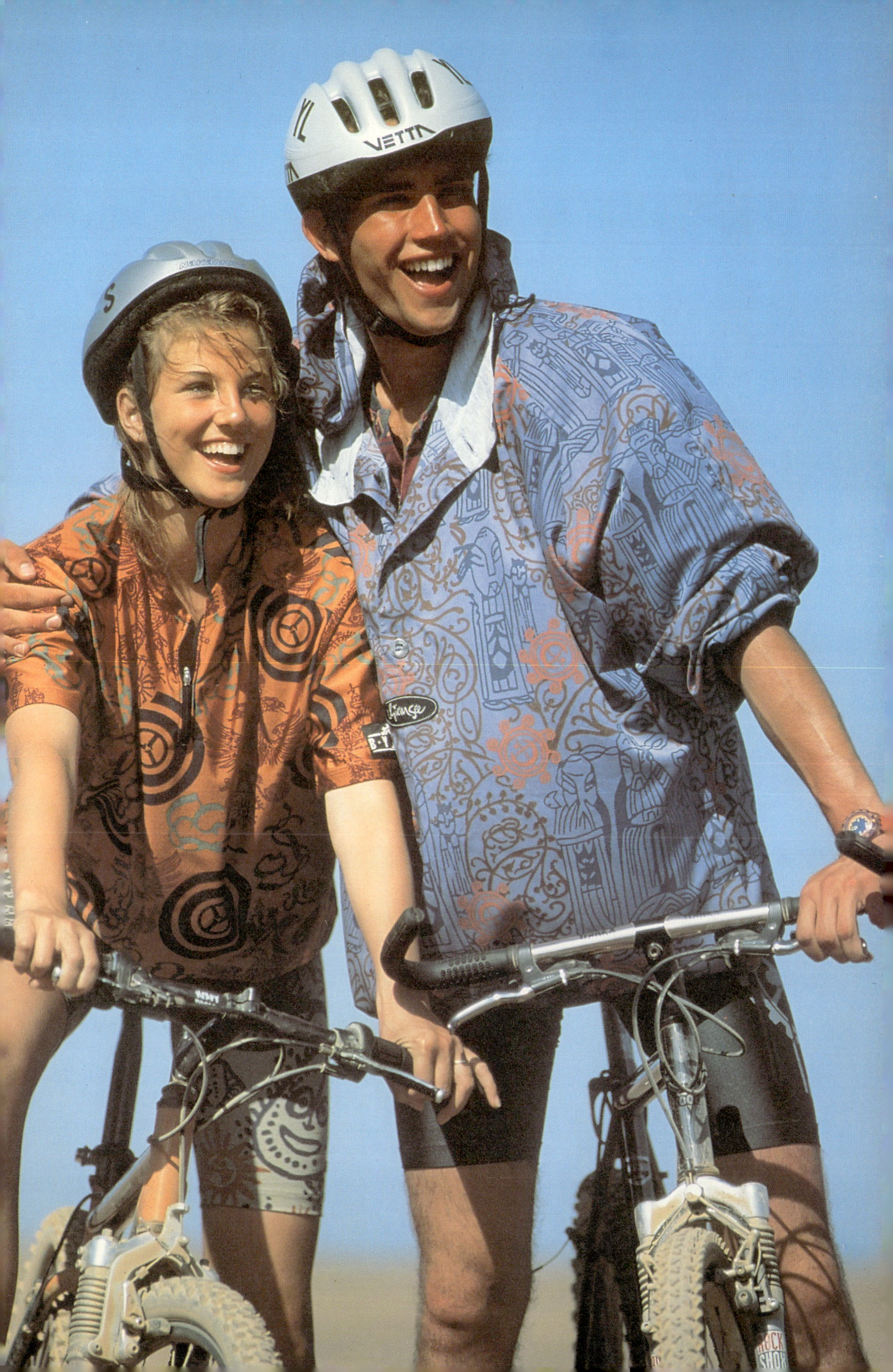
VETTA

THE SEX TEST

This is a simple true or false test to help you see what your attitudes to sex really are. Answer the questions honestly, and if you can, get a few friends to take the test too. That way you can begin to examine your own thoughts and those of others around you too. But remember — it's not our own attitudes that decide what's true and right. Sex involves basic morality, and just because we think something is right or wrong doesn't make it so!

CIRCLE TRUE OR FALSE

BASIC ATTITUDES

Sex is just for fun	T F
Sex is dirty	T F
Sex is just for making babies	T F
Sex is scary	T F
Sex is sin	T F

CHRISTIANS AND SEX

Sex is a gift from God	T F
Christians and non-Christians should see sex the same way	T F
God isn't worried about the Christian's sex life	T F
God made us sexual so it's His fault	T F
I can't help sexual temptations	T F

OUTSIDE INFLUENCES

Most people lie about their sex lives	T F
Sex is OK as long as no one gets hurt	T F
Everybody else is having sex, so what I do doesn't matter	T F
I've learned what is right and wrong about sex from friends	T F
What I read and watch affects my sexual values	T F

SEXUAL SITUATIONS

Heavy petting before marriage is wrong	T F
Feeling guilty after sex proves it was wrong	T F
Having sex is OK if you're engaged	T F
Sexual sins are very damaging	T F
To stay a virgin today is not realistic	T F

Now if you're like most people who've taken this test, you want to argue about some of the answers. Because it's true that the answer you give does depend on your situation.

For example, 'Sex is sin', depends on whether you're married or not, exactly what you mean by 'sex' (sexual intercourse, or just touching each other), and exactly what you mean by sin (is it against what God has said, or just what you might think is wrong. For example some people believe any kind of masturbation is wrong, but this is not mentioned in the Bible).

'I can't help sexual temptations', depends on whether you think temptations are wrong themselves, or whether you believe you can't help yourself, and what you should do about putting yourself into a position to get tempted! And some of the other questions may have an 'It depends' kind of answer.

But you should now have a better idea of some of the issues you need to sort out in your mind. That's what we're going to do together in this book.

OPINIONS

Take a look at some opinions on sex and see if you agree or disagree with them. Then say why and add your comments:

RACHEL
I don't know why guys have to be so <u>physical</u>. They're always pawing you about, trying to get into your underwear. They should take a cold shower and learn to control themselves.

☐ AGREE ☐ DISAGREE
COMMENTS

DEBORAH
I like the feeling of being in love, and the physical stuff of love. But I've never had sex, because I don't think it would be a good idea. I don't want to ruin my relationship with God, and I think God had some good reasons for reserving sex for marriage. My friends who have sex aren't really happy, and they get worried about getting AIDS or pregnant. I think that's really sad.

☐ AGREE ☐ DISAGREE
COMMENTS

ALICE
I don't see what the problem is. If I feel like doing it, I just do. Not with just anybody, of course, but if you like it, why deny yourself?

☐ AGREE ☐ DISAGREE
COMMENTS

REBECCA
I'm saving myself for the man I marry. I don't agree with sex before marriage, and to be honest sex doesn't really bother me. Maybe I'll find out when I get married.

☐ AGREE ☐ DISAGREE
COMMENTS

LYDIA
I think you have to let your boyfriend do what he wants. Boys can't really control themselves, and they need to get relief. So even though I don't enjoy it so much, I do it so he's happy.

☐ AGREE ☐ DISAGREE
COMMENTS

EMILY
I think sex is dirty. I don't know why we were made this way. When a boy tries to touch me, I tell him to get lost. I think all the talk about sex is wrong. From what I've heard it's overrated anyway. Just thinking about it makes me feel sick inside. I don't know if I'll ever get married.

☐ AGREE ☐ DISAGREE
COMMENTS

2

What kind of person am I?

The Lord God said, 'It is not good for the man to live alone. I will make a suitable companion to help him.' So . . . God . . . formed a woman. Genesis 2:18, 22.

WHO AM I?

A strange question, maybe. But you need to have some answers. So: take a few moments and try to *describe yourself*. Who you really are. Even write some ideas down on a piece of paper if you like. Just try to think about what kind of person you are. Are you kind, thoughtful, caring, intelligent, sad, angry, loving, upset, cold, aggressive . . . what?

Why should you want to do this? Because you need to try to understand yourself. Because if you don't, how can you expect anyone else to understand you!

Then, if you trust someone enough, you could always ask them what they think of you. What kind of personality you have. What you appear to like and dislike. Because sometimes we're so close to ourselves we don't see ourselves very well! But one of the most important needs for a good relationship is knowing yourself. So look at yourself in the mirror, and get to know who you see there.

Add to that a sense of how special you are. Maybe people put you down. Maybe others don't think much of you. But there's nobody else just like you on the whole planet. So be glad that you are made so special. Even if you don't like some things about yourself (like the shape of your nose or maybe you think your legs are fat), don't think badly about yourself. That's very important.

You will also find out more about yourself as you relate to other people. Sometimes they will tell you straight. Other times you will find out by the way they treat you. But don't let anyone treat you as if you are not important. You are!

SOMEONE TO LOVE

You will also find deep inside you a need to love and be loved. That's the way we were created. So remember your specialness, and when you

> **To be a woman is to have the same needs and longings as a man. We need love and we wish to give it. If only we all could accept that there is no difference between us where human values are concerned. Whatever sex. Whatever the life we have chosen to live.**
> LIV ULLMANN

'I just want someone to love.'

'Oh, if only there was someone I could love.'

We all look for that mutual attraction. We want to be appreciated for what we are. We look for affection — that assurance that we are special. And when we can't seem to find what we're looking for, then we suffer. We are made to love and be loved.

Most of all we want to be able to share our love with someone else; to have that mutual experience of being in love. For while it may be tragic never to find that love, it is even more tragic to find we cannot love.

We remember one girl telling us she could not love. She wasn't sure what love was; but she thought she

start looking for a boy-friend, make sure he appreciates what makes you special. And he must be special for you, too, somebody you want to love as he loves you.

The same day both a 16-year-old schoolgirl and then an 80-year-old widow told us just about the same thing:

It's healthy to stop and think about who you are and what makes you different. What sort of person will others make of you?

We all look for mutual attraction. We look for affection, to be wanted, to be assured that we are special.

was unable to love anyone. She married this last summer and tells us she's so happy. She's very much in love, and smiled when we reminded her of what she once told us.

In loving we find that we become fulfilled and our personalities develop. Because we are basically self-centred beings, to love in the right sense makes us better people. We are less concerned about ourselves, and more concerned about other people. And if this doesn't happen then, whatever you may be feeling, it isn't love. Because love puts the other person first.

WHAT LOVE DOES

That's why our ability to love shows the image of God in us. God is love, and so He made us that way. You cannot love without having someone to love! That is why God created thinking beings — ones who could reason, understand and love — and so become His loving, understanding friends.

God put in us that need to love and be loved; it's part of God's nature. If that need is not met, or is hurt or damaged, then we need God's help to make us in His image again. The Devil knows all about this — which is why he takes so much trouble to cause problems. He wants to destroy loving relationships, because they reflect the goodness and love of God Himself.

What happens when you truly love? You trust the other person, you are vulnerable, you give yourself. You desperately hope your love will be returned, but you cannot be sure. You can see why loving is often so

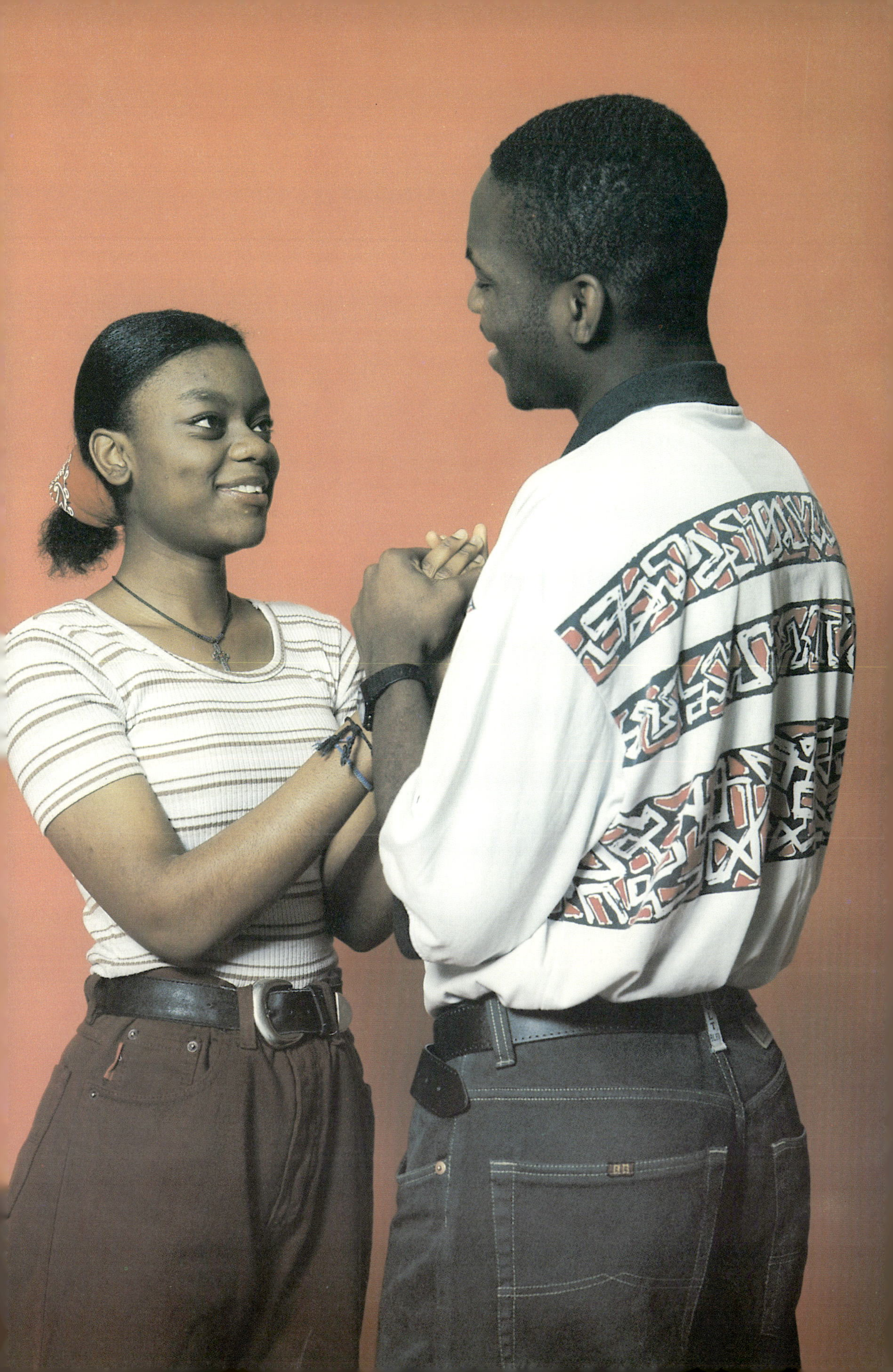

dangerous! But it is the way God treats us: He loves us, whether we love Him or not.

Some young people we've talked to want to protect themselves: 'I'll only admit so much, and see what he or she does.' Being careful may be wise, but eventually love cannot be expressed with lots of conditions. 'I'll love you if you love me!' There are no guarantees that by loving you will be loved in return. You love in hope!

No guarantees! So love faces you with many challenges, many demands. If you've been hurt in love, you may have decided, 'Never again!' But the only way to be sure that it won't happen again is to isolate yourself and not let anyone come close. That's a big price to pay. So think again, and (carefully) allow friendships to develop. And love may flower again . . . .

Of course, what we call love is far from the ideal. It's not perfect. Often some terrible things are done in the name of love. Love may hurt very much. But it is perhaps the most valuable gift that we have been given by a loving Creator. We believe it's worth saving. Don't ever give up on love, even if you never have the chance of human love. For the God of love still loves you with an undying love . . . .

You may still be wondering exactly what this love means. We can do no better than refer you to these words:

'Love is patient and kind; it is not jealous or conceited or proud; love

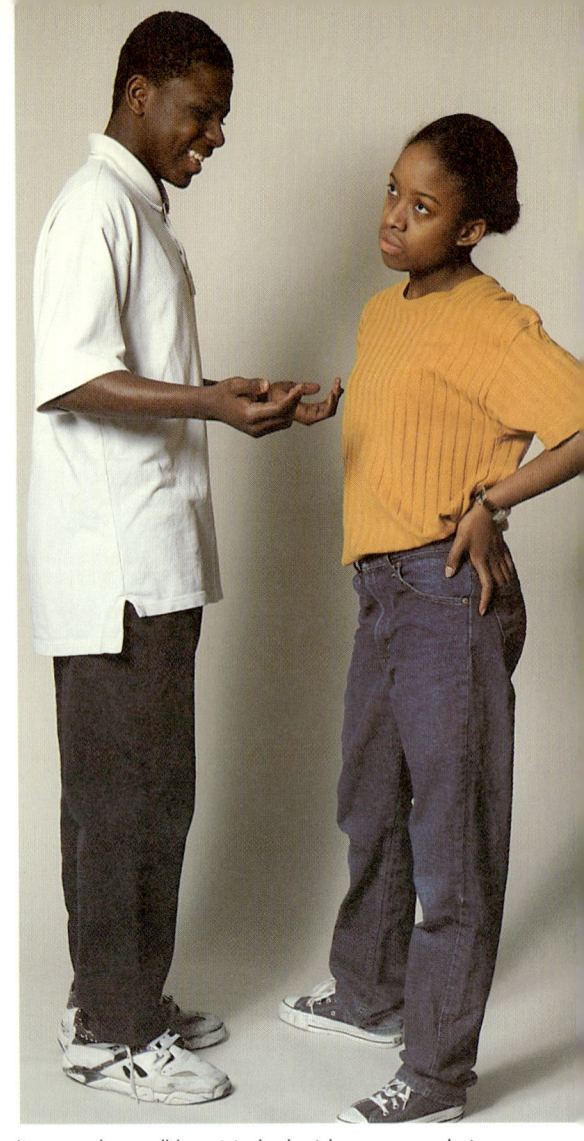

It seems impossible not to be hurt by someone, but it won't help if you isolate yourself and refuse friendships to avoid being hurt again.

is not ill-mannered or selfish or irritable; love does not keep a record of wrongs; love is not happy with evil, but is happy with the truth. Love never gives up; and its faith, hope, and patience never fail.' (1 Corinthians 13:4-7.)

RELATE

So let's think about how we relate. To ourselves, to one another, and to God. And remember, this applies to all our relationships, not just with boy-friends. You can make a list of what RELATE stands for, like this:

R — Respond
E — Experience
L — Listen
A — Act
T — Talk
E — Enjoy

RESPOND

You cannot have a relationship with a rock — at least not a very meaningful one! A relationship means that you respond to each other. One of the great mistakes couples make is to forget to respond to one another. You take each other for granted. You don't think of what the other is saying or doing. You must show yourself *responsive* — that you really do care about the other. And in love, the other person comes first.

EXPERIENCE

You must share time together. Building experiences together is central to any relationship. Funny situations you can laugh about (maybe only afterwards!). Facing life in partnership demands that you do not live separately. You must be involved in each other's interests. You try to feel how the other feels, you want to understand the inner life of the other. You share one another's problems, at school or home, talking them through calmly so that the problem 'cools down', rather than being 'blown up'.

LISTEN

Listening comes before talking. You may be tempted to rush in and say something — and all too often to regret what you said. One piece of good advice is, before you fire off a stinging remark to count to ten. We would add to that: and once you've got to ten, keep counting! In a poll of what people appreciate in their friends, being a good listener came right up near the top in most responses. And it's not just saying, 'Uh-huh. I hear you. Oh,

Too many relationships are permanently damaged or destroyed by that ill-advised cutting remark.

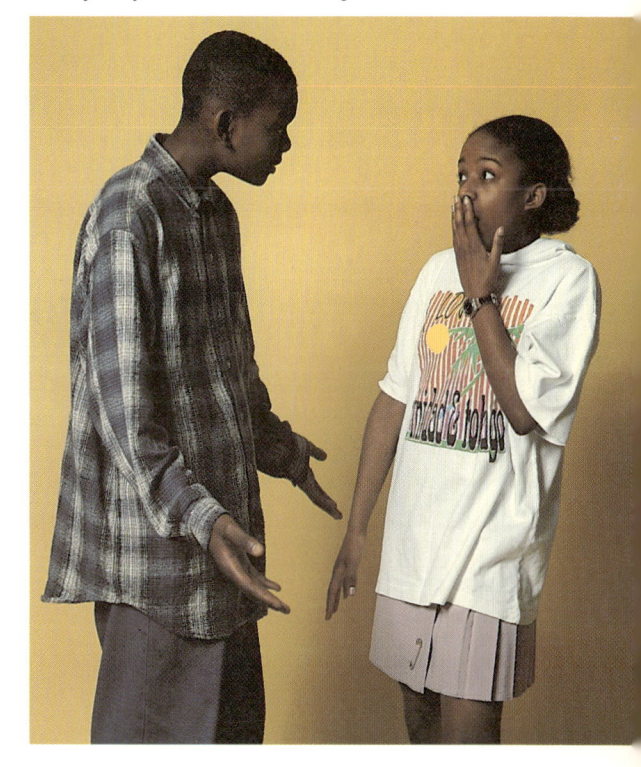

26

Get involved in one another's interests, enjoy sharing together the good times, the funny situations, the difficult decisions . . . .

really . . . .' *True listening means seeking to sympathize, to understand, and to help.*

ACT

You have to *do* something. If you don't like the situation, CHANGE IT! You do not have to just sit there. Your boy-friend needs to know what you really want — don't let him try to guess what you're thinking. (Men can be very insensitive at times!) All too often girls have told us that they suffered in silence for as long as they could, and then blew up. You need to do something *before* the situation gets to that stage. Love is not being passive, allowing the other person to do just as he pleases. That is not helpful to him either. You and your thoughts and your values are equally important. For a relationship to succeed, you need to know that what you do makes a difference.

TALK

Yes, once you've listened, talk. Communication breakdown destroys more relationships than adultery or money worries or career moves or anything else. It's an easy habit to fall into; you're tired of arguing, so you give up. Or you sulk to punish him. Or you think there's nothing left to say. DON'T YOU BELIEVE IT! If you love, (or loved — for love can be resurrected), then speak about your concerns, honestly and carefully without getting angry. (At least don't get angry too often. Sometimes getting angry is important, too, for it shows him how much you really do feel.) Make sure you talk through the happy times, too, sharing the wonder of life together.

ENJOY

Oh, how important! Sometimes we treat love and sex and relationships so very *seriously* that we forget to enjoy them. You can't get all your information from text books (not even this one!). That's often the trouble with sex manuals — they're like mechanical instruction booklets. And if you followed them in a step-by-step manner (like some cooking recipe) then all the joy and fun would soon be gone. A great part of falling in love is the journey of discovery together. Learn as you share together, and remember to include the God who gave us real joy.

COMMUNICATION

All of these six aspects are essential to a good relationship. They prove that good communication is vital for you to develop and maintain a two-way understanding

Think of some of the barriers to good and effective communication. You can be speaking different languages even when you're each using the same words. You can say something and mean something different. You can pretend to be listening when you're not. You can refuse to speak about certain things . . . .

EXPERIMENTS

Try these four experiments:

▶ Talk to another person (maybe your boy-friend) about one subject, and have the other person speak on a totally different subject back to you. Neither should respond to what the other says, but simply continue with their own subject. It's hard to do when you try! — but so many people operate this way in their relationships.

▶ One person is the speaker, the other silent. The speaker is to try and gain some kind of response

To love is to share. Talk, even when there's tension or disagreement. Lack of communication destroys relationships.

from the other, who tries to make no response whatsoever. Again, when you consciously try to do this, it is difficult. But this situation is commonplace in many relationships.

▶ Ask your boy-friend to say something about you to you. Then repeat the same for him. Interestingly, most comments will be appreciative and positive. And frequently these comments are never actually said — for a variety of reasons — and yet they are so important. However, in stale relationships, the comments will often be negative.

▶ Share some vital truth about yourself with each other. By thinking about doing this it shows the kind of trust you need to have in each other. How sure are you that you can confide in each other?

You can apply these lessons about communication to all relationships. Most of all, the need to communicate properly must be there. How stupid it is to communicate and not worry about whether you are understood correctly or not!

See how important this is in planning who to spend your life with? For how will it ever happen — knowing me, knowing you — if the real, sincere and deep communication isn't there?

KNOWING ME

So OK, maybe I've thought about the kind of person I am. But where do all these feelings come from? Why do my emotions seem to take control? Why do my clear determinations turn to jelly when I look into his eyes?

Part of the answer comes from the physical processes that are going on inside your body, especially since puberty. That mix of hormones and biochemicals that is making you a woman, the onset of monthly periods, the glandular activity — all those amazing changes that are part of maturing — affect to some degree the way you operate. Of course, if you're asking us to explain exactly why we love then we can't. But it is part of God's plan for us to mature and develop into human beings who are attracted to others, to become sexual.

Sex is part of who you are. It is not wrong, or filthy, or dirty. You have been made by God to experience pleasure — to become physically stimulated, to enjoy another's touch, kiss, caress, and to want to give the same in return.

Since sex is a most wonderful part of you, it shouldn't be thrown away. Virginity is not lost, it is given. And it should be a very special present to the one you truly love and trust. Sometimes your 'desires' — the physical emotions that are a mixture of how you think and how your body feels — try to carry you away. That's natural, too, but this should only happen when it's safe. It's a bit like the thrill you have when you're on a roller-coaster. In that situation (hopefully) the excitement is safe.

You might have the same thrill(!) when the car you're travelling in rushes down a hill and the brakes fail. But the end result will be very different . . . .

If your feelings do carry you away, and you act unwisely, all is not lost. It doesn't mean you are damaged goods, or worthless, or that you have to continue down the slippery slope. Damaged emotions can be healed, false experiences can be turned around, your life can be rescued. God can do it. But it is always so much better to stay in control and know what you can and cannot do.

SEX AND WASHING MACHINES?

Take your average washing machine. Even the most untrained person knows you're not supposed to wash your socks with your blouse. There are rules. But these rules are more like common sense. Somebody didn't get up in Parliament and make up these 'Washing machine laws'. You use your washing machine properly because you want the right result. Now think about such rules and apply them to sex.

Would you put your washing machine on spin cycle for hours and then wonder why it broke? Similarly, don't rev up your sexual motor. Don't allow yourself to get into a sexual spin where you'll lose your head.

You don't put everything in the boil wash either! Living in red-hot

It's great to enjoy the attentions of a partner, God designed it that way, but it's necessary to stay in-control.

sexual excitement can only lead one way. Cool down, and avoid 'hot' situations.

You make sure you read the labels on your clothes, don't you? To see which ones to bleach, or which are delicates, how hot the water should be and so on? Why not read your own label? See your own directions from the Maker as to sexual behaviour. We are all different, so make sure you know how to handle yourself — and your boy-friend!

Don't put in too much soap and get yourself into a sexual lather! A lot of bubbles may be fun at first,

SELF-WORTH

Score yourself on this test. Do it honestly, for you want to know more about yourself and how this can be changed for the better.

*Score 1 for Disagree   2 for Maybe Disagree   3 for Don't Know
          4 for Maybe Agree   5 for Agree*

- ☐ I feel happy about myself.
- ☐ I think other people appreciate the kind of person I am.
- ☐ I take criticism well.
- ☐ I'm not upset if I don't get praise due to me.
- ☐ What I know about myself is more important than what others say about me.
- ☐ It's not what I do that makes me valuable, it's what I am.
- ☐ I don't expect to fail, I just do my best.
- ☐ I don't worry too much about my image.
- ☐ I know and accept both my abilities and my failings.
- ☐ I know I am special in God's eyes.

A very low score shows you have some definite problems in the way you see yourself. You are marking yourself down, and don't rate yourself at all. It's not easy to change, but you must have some help in seeing that you are a valuable person, and that God sees you as special.

A high score tends to indicate that you are well-balanced and have a good perception of yourself. However, an almost perfect score may also indicate that you are perhaps somewhat arrogant — you can take self-worth too far!

---

but not when they spread all over the kitchen floor. Sexual 'fun' can take a lot of mopping up . . . .

And you can think of some more comparisons.

KNOWING YOURSELF

Think seriously about these ideas. Know yourself — and you'll avoid many difficulties. All too often girls tell us, 'I didn't know what I was doing.' That can be a cop-out, but it can also be true. So know *beforehand* what you're going to do. If you do love, then you are making choices, and you need to choose right!

Way back at the beginning of time (for humanity, at least) God looked at the aloneness of man (we don't want to say loneliness, that would be different). In contrast to everything else — everything that 'was good' — God said that this was *not* good. And this experience of being alone was before Adam's sin!

So God must have created hu-

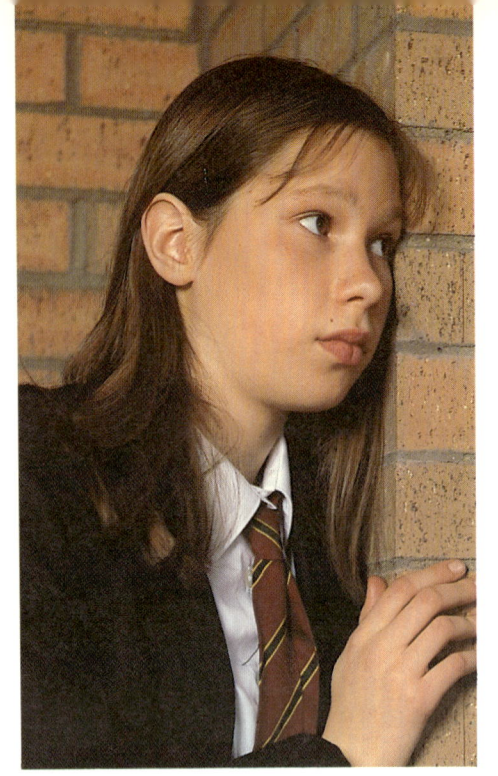

Damaged emotions can be healed, it's not a catastrophe, but it's best to make the right choice and avoid the temptation in the first place.

manity imperfect for Him to say it was 'not good'? No. God had simply created Adam with the need for another's company, and even God's company was not enough. God had made man with the need for company. God never intended our lives to be lived on our own. We are made for each other.

Thank God for who you are, and for being able to love and be loved. 'Dear friends, let us love one another, because love comes from God. Whoever loves is a child of God and knows God. Whoever does not love does not know God . . . .' (1 John 4:7, 8.)

HOW I SEE MYSELF — THE 49 STEPS

Here's a list of 49 different personal qualities.
Tick the words that you think apply to you personally right now:

- ☐ kind
- ☐ harsh
- ☐ loveable
- ☐ silly
- ☐ attractive
- ☐ cruel
- ☐ happy
- ☐ thoughtful
- ☐ lonely
- ☐ caring
- ☐ depressed
- ☐ intelligent
- ☐ sad
- ☐ pleasant
- ☐ sexual
- ☐ selfish
- ☐ angry
- ☐ wise
- ☐ mean
- ☐ friendly
- ☐ upset
- ☐ foolish
- ☐ good
- ☐ cold
- ☐ aggressive
- ☐ inhibited
- ☐ clever
- ☐ obedient
- ☐ ignorant
- ☐ cheerful
- ☐ greedy
- ☐ sensible
- ☐ bitter
- ☐ reserved
- ☐ generous
- ☐ bad
- ☐ considerate
- ☐ gentle
- ☐ sensitive
- ☐ charming
- ☐ affectionate
- ☐ irritable
- ☐ stupid
- ☐ decent
- ☐ sympathetic
- ☐ quarrelsome
- ☐ helpful
- ☐ passionate
- ☐ extrovert

QUESTIONS AND ANSWERS

I'm a young woman in the church. I would like to marry a Christian but I can't find any available ones. What should I do?

The sexual imbalance (we mean in numbers!) is a frequent concern in churches. In many denominations women outnumber men by two to one. This will obviously cause problems when it comes to finding a suitable partner, and various responses are clear: some look outside the church, others try different churches in their search; while some (either by choice or circumstance) never marry at all.

Enjoy the company of a teen group of boys and girls and find out how they 'tick'.

So what should you do? Firstly, marrying is not the greatest objective — especially if it means compromising what you believe. But you can make sure that you have many opportunities to meet Christian men: attendance at Christian conferences, camps, retreats, study groups and so on. Not that you are deliberately husband hunting, of course, just expanding your circle of friends. You might also date non-Christians, but be aware of the potential dangers and the need for a firm commitment to your Christian principles before ever considering a more serious relationship. Examples of 'romance evangelism' do exist, but there are various difficulties too. Most of all, let the Lord lead and guide you, and don't make marriage your single life-goal.

When should I start dating boys?

I doubt anyone can make any definite rule about what age is right. Much depends on the maturity of the person, her sense of responsibility, and the setting. In some cultures there are set procedures, in others not. Once puberty begins the process of physical maturing, there's a new interest in the opposite sex. And there is certainly nothing wrong in beginning friendships right then, though to call this dating may not be the right term. More important than dating one person is to go out in a mixed group and discover the way in which boys and girls relate to one another. Discuss this with an adult — preferably your parents, or some other trustworthy and responsible person. Then when you are sure you can handle the situation, and you feel personally ready for a more specific girl-boy relationship, then you can begin dating — going out together. Be sure not to be pressurized by people around you though, and don't worry if you're not dating when others are.

Why are some men and women less sensual than others?

None of us is made the same. It would be really boring if we were, wouldn't it? The fact that we are each unique means that the possibilities for mutual discovery and interaction are limitless. However, the very fact that we are different can also lead to misunderstandings and complications, especially when it comes to sex. The libido, or sex drive, varies from person to person. Why? Well, that's a bit like asking why some people are at their best in the morning, and others in the evening; or why some people are better runners than others. Much has to do with heredity, and also with the way that we have grown up. However, sensuality is not perhaps the single most important factor here. In a truly loving relationship there is a meeting of minds and bodies, a process of accepting the other for what they are. So if one is more or less sensual than the other, then in love they take that into account and readjust their behaviour accordingly. In our experience physical desires of both partners eventually settle down to some kind of norm and this is not a major problem.

Is the felt-need for sex the same in both males and females?

This question follows on from the previous one, although this is more general. A wide spectrum of physical response occurs in both sexes, however it is also true that this sexual response does vary between the sexes. In a later chapter we will look at some of these differences. The general assumption is that men need sex more than women, and there are perhaps some physiological reasons for this. But to suggest that men cannot control their sexual drive while women can is to fall into the sexual double-standard which is as much advanced by women as men. Some men do, of course, suggest that they *have* to be satisfied, but this is more a device to achieve what they want than scientific fact. Perhaps the best answer is to say that as a generalization males and females both have a felt-need for sex, but that this need (or drive) is expressed in different ways.

What do I do when I am friendly to a person of the opposite sex and it is interpreted as something more than just being friendly? Especially when I am not aware of showing signs of being more than friends with the other person.

Unfortunately that's a major hazard we all face! The possibility of being misunderstood is always there, and while you can try not to say or do anything that can be misconstrued, you can't necessarily avoid it. From what you say, it seems that since you're not aware of being more than normally friendly then some are *wanting* to misunderstand your friendliness. Some guys use this technique to imply that they're not the ones chasing — they were only responding to your 'come on'. But if you are *sure* you didn't intend anything, then don't feel pressured or obligated or embarrassed. To react by becoming less than your friendly self would be tragic, although you might want to check with some female friends you trust that you're not unconsciously flirting, or in any way (by the way you act or dress, for example) giving the wrong impression.

Should I have a list of my ideal marriage partner's characteristics?

Maybe — but not as a check list! Remember, reality may be a long way from the ideal; and you don't want to make up a husband description that is impossible to meet. I think you should have some idea of what you enjoy and appreciate in a man, and not just physically, either. You know yourself, your attitudes, beliefs and interests;

and in some way your partner should complement these. But don't make a rigorous catalogue, or spend too much time checking how each potential boy-friend scores on your wish list . . . .

Why do I feel the way I do? Sometimes I'm just so hyped up, and other times I don't seem to feel anything.

You don't give much detail about what and why you are feeling as you do. We all go through different experiences that affect us in a whole variety of ways, so it's hard to be precise based on what you've asked. But you should be aware of body cycles — the changes that occur in your physical system, particularly to do with your monthly period. Sometimes before and during a period you can feel irritable or sad. This is often called pre-menstrual tension or PMT, and is recognized as a very real symptom nowadays. If it is severe, then go and see your doctor. Other chemical and hormonal changes also occur that can affect your emotional state, and if they seem to be quite regular then again these may be linked to the reproductive cycle. You don't say whether you are particularly bothered by this, but you need to be aware of how your feelings can be affected — since you may be particularly vulnerable to situations, either when you're hyped up or when you feel low.

I have some weird dreams that I think are due to bad thoughts. What can I do about this?

None of us can actually control

When your body cycles begin they can affect your moods, often resulting in being irritable or depressed.

what we dream. I know good Christians who tell me they never deliberately concentrate on bad subjects yet still have nightmares. So you cannot feel responsible for dreams. That said, you must also be sure that you are not contributing to them by concentrating on inappropriate ideas and thoughts when you are awake. Every Christian must guard the 'avenue of the soul' — what goes into the mind. So be careful what TV you watch, the books you read, the pictures you see — and the fantasies you allow yourself. If you are conscious of dwelling on what you call bad thoughts then read Philippians 4:8: 'Fill your minds with those things that are good and that deserve praise: things that are true, noble, right, pure, lovely, and honourable.' Instead of stamping evil out, crowd it out with good!

3

What about me, physically?

You created every part of me; you put me together in my mother's womb. Psalm 139:13.

YOUR SEXUALITY

So let's get down to it. What about your sexuality? How does all this work, physically?

Before we go any further, we need to strike some kind of balance. This is not a sex textbook. But neither is it some old-fashioned book that talks mysteriously about 'passing on the torch of life' or about 'feminine concerns'. What we'll do is speak openly and honestly about the physical body, including the sexual organs, that God gave us.

BECOMING A WOMAN

Now let's explain about becoming a woman. Your body is a wonderful creation, and it helps a lot to understand what's going on. You may also want to take a closer look at yourself in a mirror since then you can see what we are talking about.

Briefly these are the changes that happen in growing from a child to a woman. (The words in brackets are the correct medical terms, and it is helpful to know these. Some of the foolishness talked about sex is expressed in all those silly names for the sex organs and so on.)

If you've passed through puberty, you'll know that your body has changed. Your breasts have developed, your pubic hair has grown (and under your arms), your hips have broadened. You will also have begun to have periods, the discharge of waste blood and tissue through your vagina. This is part of the preparation made for reproduction, so that you can have a baby.

What is happening inside is that every month or so (periods are not always regular, especially at the beginning) your ovary releases an egg (ovum) which moves down through the reproductive system to the womb (uterus). If it is fertilized by a male cell (sperm) then this egg will grow into a baby — in nine months or so.

If fertilization does not occur,

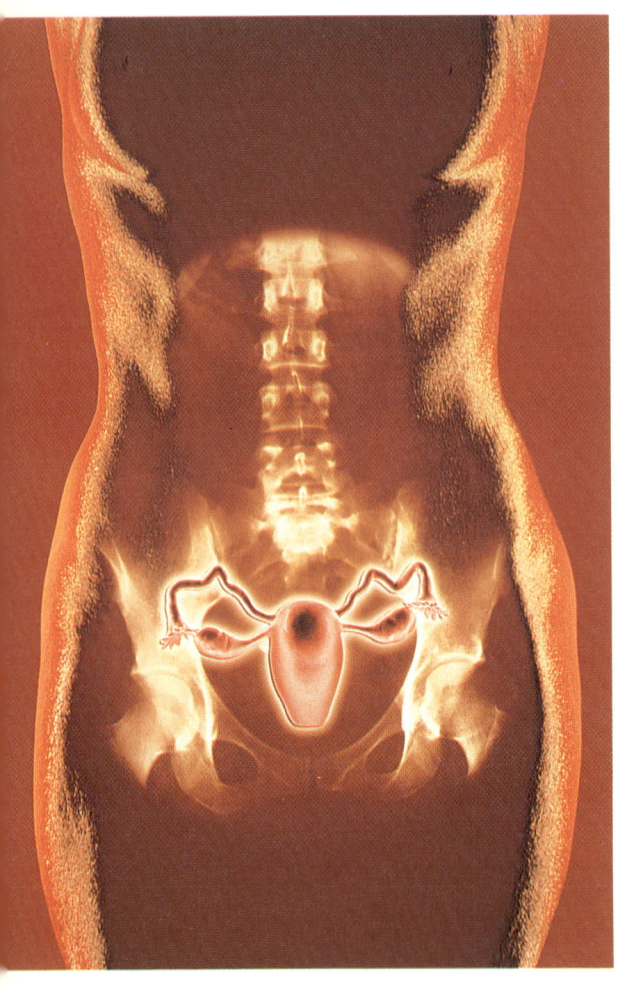

This shows the position of the female reproductive system within the pelvis.

particularly heavy or painful, you should discuss this with your mother or family doctor or some other adult you respect and trust (preferably female). Be careful during your periods to take special care of yourself.

Remember: for you to become pregnant sperm must enter your uterus, for it is only when sperm from the male comes into contact with an egg that conception (making a baby) can occur. This doesn't necessarily mean you must have had full sexual intercourse to become pregnant. If semen (the fluid containing sperm) from the male is spilt near the entrance to the vagina, it is possible for some sperm to swim up to the uterus.

All that may sound a bit complicated. So take a look at the pictures which make it much clearer.

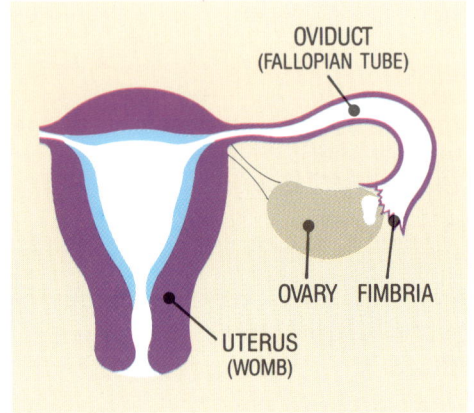

then the soft cushion of tissue and its blood supply that lines the womb is shed; this is what you notice as your period (menstruation). You will be using either sanitary pads or tampons to take care of this discharge from your vagina. If you have any questions or concerns about your periods, especially if they seem

The illustration above shows you how all your parts fit together in what is called 'the reproductive organs'. That means the parts of your body which are designed for having babies. You can see the ovaries that produce the tiny egg. An egg is produced every month once you start having periods. This egg passes down the fallopian tubes into the womb (uterus). If sperms are present (from having sex) then the egg is fertilized and attaches to the wall of the uterus, and eventually grows into a baby.

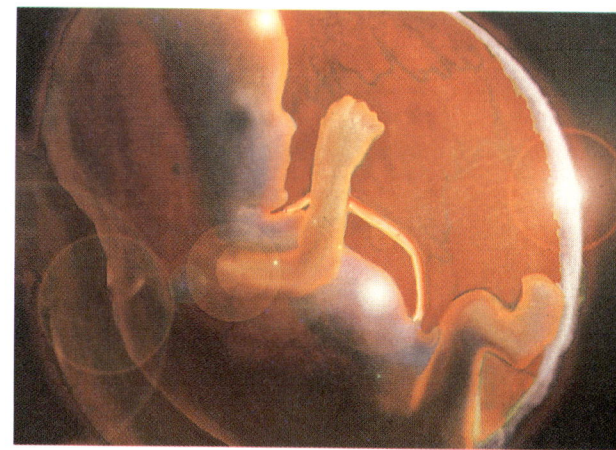

After five months the foetus has now developed into a fully formed infant.

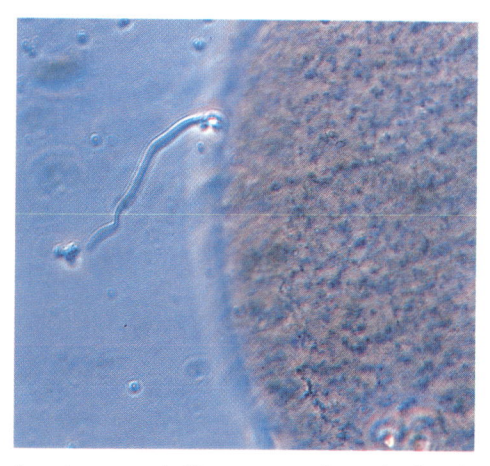

A male sperm fertilizes an egg from the female ovary.

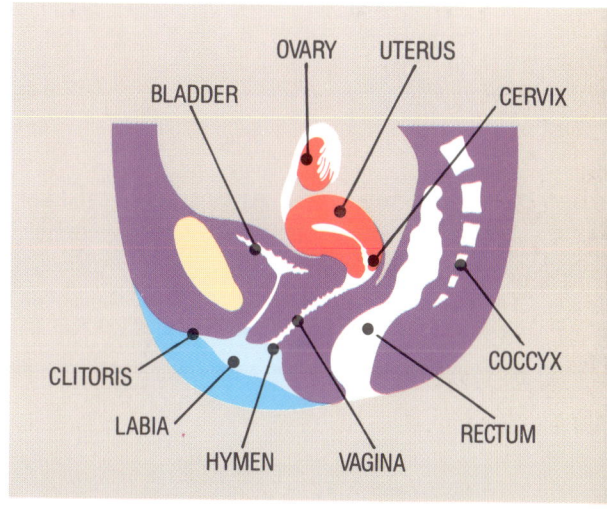

A cross section through the vagina and the uterus — as if you were looking from one side.

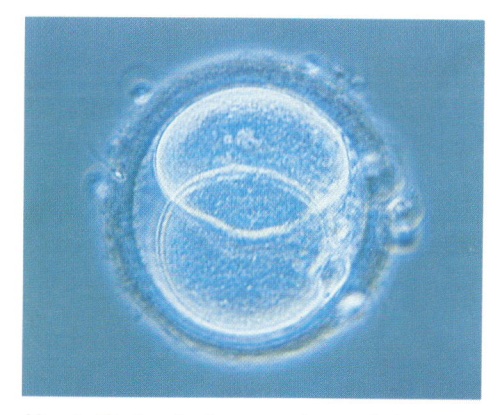

After fertilization the human embryo called a zygote starts dividing into multiple cells.

In the illustration above you can see the lips (labia) that surround the opening to the vagina. At the top you can see a little 'button' which is the clitoris. This organ is very sensitive and is what produces pleasant feelings when it is stimulated. The clitoris is stimulated during sexual

HOW FERTILIZATION OCCURS

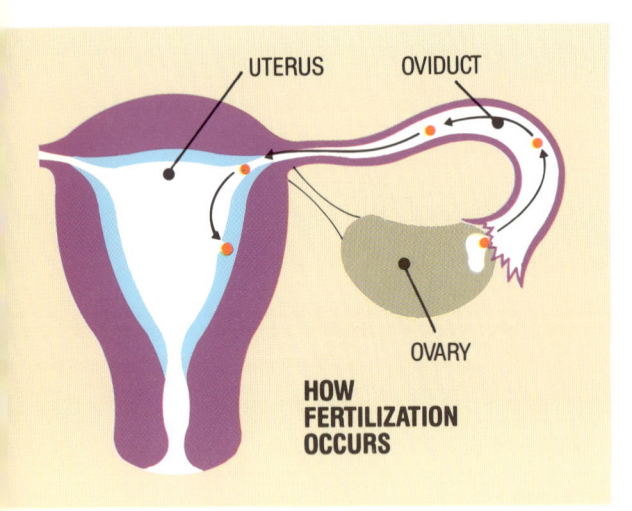

An egg leaves the ovary and travels up the oviduct (fallopian tube) where fertilization occurs if a male sperm is present. It is then carried into the uterus to become embedded in its lining. Here the embryo develops into a baby.

intercourse, and can produce what is called an orgasm — a strong feeling of pleasure. Inside the vagina you can also see the small opening through which urine passes.

Inside the vagina is lined with rippled tissue which expands and becomes lubricated during sexual activity. This helps during sexual intercourse when the penis enters the vagina.

Sometimes the vagina has its internal opening partially closed by a thin membrane called the hymen. This is broken when sexual intercourse is begun, and there may be some bleeding. This is associated with losing your virginity. At some times and in some cultures this was seen as very important. But the hymen is not always present, or is not extensive. Also the use of tampons may already have broken the hymen, or it may have been lost in some other way (some suggest horse riding, for example). So it doesn't mean you are not a virgin just because you don't have a hymen or don't bleed during your first intercourse. This needs to be explained to your future husband before the wedding night to avoid misunderstandings.

THE SEXUAL ACT

What is all this for? You've seen the pictures, but maybe you wonder how it all works in practice.

How does 'it' all happen? Maybe we can leave the medical aspects, which make it sound rather clinical. How does making love start?

You have probably already experienced the beginnings of all this — for it starts with touching. The delight of touch has been with you from infancy. You may kiss your mother or other family members — you certainly shake hands!

If you have (or had) a boy-friend, holding hands is often the first step. It is part of physical closeness, the stimulation of caresses. You may even get excited by someone stroking your little finger! The body reacts to such stimulation, and you may respond. At first touching is limited to hands and face, but then this moves on to other parts of the body.

Kissing is the same. What begins as a quick peck on the cheek moves on to kissing on the mouth, kissing

Holding, touching, kissing is the start of a progression which is designed to bring great pleasure but which is also difficult to stop.

with the mouth open, touching tongues and so on. What is important to recognize is that there is a chain. One thing literally does lead to another. So don't fool yourself that you can leave it all open — you need to decide *in advance* how far is enough. Your body won't make that choice for you — quite the opposite.

According to many studies, the physical progression from here leads to:

- more and heavier kissing and cuddling
- petting (touching breasts and genitals through clothes)
- heavy petting (the direct stimulation of breasts and genitals), mutual masturbation
- sexual intercourse

Obviously this progression leads to actions that are wrong for the Christian outside of marriage. The Bible does not draw an exact line here, but we believe that once genital contact is made then it becomes increasingly difficult to resist the desire for sexual intercourse.

The process of sexual intercourse involves many of the actions mentioned above — the kissing and cuddling and mutual stimulation prepares the body for the action of the man putting his penis into the woman's vagina. Then by thrusting (pushing the penis in and out) the man is stimulated to orgasm and his semen shoots out from his penis into the woman's vagina, near the entrance to the uterus. The woman may also experience an orgasm in the process, particularly if the man makes sure to stimulate the clitoris. (An orgasm is an intense feeling of pleasure that makes your whole body tingle, and is accompanied by muscle spasms in the genital area. Someone once described it as the feeling you get just before you sneeze! Another explained that it's like a good explosion.)

Afterwards there is a period of rest and recovery. All too often instead of mutual satisfaction, this is the time for self-doubt and despair among those whose relationships are not as they should be. This so-called post-coital depression is much sadder when the thought, 'this is wrong', should have been made some minutes earlier. Don't get yourself into a situation in which the beauty of pleasure is destroyed by the pain of regret.

CONSEQUENCES

The consequences of sexual intercourse need to be mentioned briefly. Obviously, there is the chance of becoming pregnant. In a marriage, that is a pleasant thought. Not so if you are a young teenager still at school. To decide to take precautions is not the answer, for not only are they not 100 per cent effective, they can't prevent the sadness and guilt.

Then there's the risk of diseases, especially AIDS. We'll look in more detail at these very real dangers later on. But nobody in today's society should be in ignorance as to the gamble they take in sexual activity. The answer is not in safe sex but in following God's good advice.

But more than any of this the real reason not to indulge in sex should be because it will hurt you as a person and your relationship to your loving Lord. It will also affect the other person in the same way. As

Pregnancy is a great experience — to those within a stable marriage relationship. Otherwise it can be devastating — for you and the baby.

we've already seen, and will look at some more in the next chapter, God is not anti-sex. He just wants you to have the best, and not the messed-up version of sex that the world tries to sell you.

GOD OF SEX

A good way of thinking about whether your sexuality is wrong, bad, or dirty, is to think of how God sees you. Doesn't God see everything? The thought may be embarrassing at first, but since God has seen you naked every day, do you think He's offended?

LINKS IN THE SEX-CHAIN

Join up the different links to make the chain. This shows how each action leads on from the one before, and connects to the next one.

- Deep kissing
- Touching breasts
- Holding hands
- Touching genitals
- Touching arms and face
- Sexual intercourse
- Kissing
- Eye contact

Didn't He make you?

David says to God: 'For you created my inmost being; you knit me together in my mother's womb. I praise you because I am fearfully and wonderfully made . . . .' (Psalm 139:13, 14, NIV.)

Fearfully and wonderfully made. God has made you, including your breasts, your vagina, your clitoris. In fact, think of that little organ. The clitoris has no other function than as a means of gaining pleasure. Imagine it — God gave that to you, and it shows that He certainly doesn't have a down on sex or physical enjoyment. Sex isn't part of the Fall of mankind — it's nothing to do with apples! The abuse of sex that came as part of evil is just part of what sin really is: selfishness. If we use sex just to please ourselves, to take what we want, to slake our own desires — then we show ourselves to be slaves of sin.

But if our sexuality is as God intended — a giving to the other, more concerned to please than be pleased — then we will have a higher, better pleasure than just making sure we have an orgasm. True love is about giving, and in giving we receive so much more.

SO WHAT ABOUT HIM?

Him — the guy. You need to understand his sexuality too. The male sexual response is usually triggered much more quickly, and this may surprise you. The male mind (or hormones, or sex drive — whatever idea you want to use here) is quickly stimulated by visual images. You may find it impossible to believe that your boy-friend is sexually aroused just by seeing you in a miniskirt, but it happens. Men are made to respond to what they see as female attractiveness, and what you may think is nothing may be electrifying to them.

Of course, that doesn't mean you

have to make sure you dress in a black smock and put a ski-mask on! But be aware of what you are revealing and what effect this may have. Now this is no excuse for your boy-friend to blame you if something happens. He has responsibility too. But knowing how easily the male sexual response is turned on may help you. Misunderstandings will always happen, but if you can talk about them, this will help your relationship enormously.

Males may be turned on by short skirts, low tops, skimpy bikinis and so on. One girl who came to church in a see-through blouse with no bra said she was offended by all the looks she got. She felt the boys should have been able to concentrate on the service. Maybe they should. But there's also the point about making your weaker brother stumble.

If, however, your boy-friend does become stimulated and his penis becomes hard (an erection), be careful not to fall into the trap of thinking either that you are necessarily to blame, or that you have to take care of it. Erections are not always due to a sexual situation (indeed some men frequently wake up with an erection); and to attempt to blame you can be a way to invite sexual activity (like you masturbating him

You can still look attractive without the need to raise the blood pressure of the nearest male by wearing skimpy outfits.

to orgasm). Even if you *do* feel in some way responsible, is it wise to go further?

CONCERN OVER APPEARANCES

The way that women are thought of means that you may be worried about the way you look. Are you thinking: 'My breasts are too small, too big, wrongly-shaped'? Or 'I wish I had a figure like this magazine model'? Or 'Why can't I look like my best friend? She always gets the boys . . . .'?

Your physical 'equipment' may be the first thing that a boy will notice (remember what we said before about visual images). But you have to help him get past that! For you cannot be happily in love with an image; love is for the person, not the image. Certainly make the best of yourself; dressing badly and deciding not to wash isn't going to help you! But neither is going over the top in trying to look seductive.

Remember to keep your life in balance. There's more to happiness than having an immediate boyfriend. You have a whole world to explore, a full life to live, a career to enjoy. And being happy but single is far better than married and bitter.

For if you're really looking for a life partner, the fact that you don't look like those models in the glossy magazines isn't going to be a major problem. Beauty fades, bodies age — but a fulfilled relationship will, with God, last forever.

QUESTIONS AND ANSWERS

Are some women born frigid?

Frigidity — the lack of sexual response, or its repression — is not really to do with the way you are born but with experience. A woman who has associated sex with bad incidents in her life, or who has been taught that sex is disgusting, may become frigid in her relationships with men and, in particular, with her husband. Another factor is that we differ in our degree of sexual drive (sometimes called libido). For some people, both men and women, sex is just not that important, and this may indeed be the way they are made.

But your question is perhaps due to concerns you have over your own sexuality, and not having anyone else to compare yourself with. Certainly the fact that you don't get turned on as quickly as your boyfriend doesn't make you frigid, just normal! And if he has suggested this, then he may be trying to force the pace by implying that you are not as responsive as he wants. To over-react and say to yourself, 'I'll show him I'm not frigid' would be playing right into his hands — and could be disastrous for both of you. It may also just be that you are not really in love.

My boy-friend says when he has a hard-on he has to get relief. Is this true?

No. An erection may be uncomfortable. But an erection is only due to blood filling the penis due to some kind of excitation. Obviously if that is the result of something you are doing, then stop! The penis will return to normal in due course. And don't be pressurized into going further, because he's obviously wanting you either to masturbate him to climax (orgasm) or to have sexual intercourse in order to satisfy his sexual urge. Getting into this kind of situation (which will then be repeated) will change your relationship.

Can a woman with very minute breasts enjoy sex as well as the woman with large breasts?

Breast size has nothing to do with sexual enjoyment. The source of pleasure is in the nerve endings, not in the size. Some men do have a complex over large breasts, and *they* may enjoy sex more. This just shows that much of sexual enjoyment is in the mind — what you think and fantasize about. But if you have smaller breasts, this should not lead you to think that your pleasure will be in any way reduced. Certainly we would not suggest any surgery to increase breast size, as this may even make your breasts less responsive. There is no evidence that creams supposed to improve your bust size actually work either. So be happy as you are — and remember that smaller breasts may be better for breast-feeding infants than larger ones.

What is an organism?

We think the word you really mean is 'orgasm'. You've probably heard people talking about it, and wondered what they were talking about. In today's world, a great deal is made of achieving orgasm through sex. For some women, this is the great objective, and has been termed the Big 'O'. This simply shows an obsession that probably makes things worse, not better.

For men, an orgasm is associated with semen leaving the penis (ejaculation). In women, this physical sensation that has been described as 'feeling I'm about to explode' is generally associated with stimulation of the clitoris, either during intercourse or oral sex/masturbation. Some women never have this experience, but still have very happy and satisfied sexual lives. For others, they may not experience this for years. From those who have spoken to us, it would seem that usually a wholly comfortable situation of loving trust must be present, and the man must learn how to please his wife. But this is something that is part of discovery for you with your husband, and don't let anyone rob you of this journey together.

Is it true that the size of an erected penis is 15cm (6")?

Penis size varies somewhat, but not a great deal. Fifteen centimetres may be seen as average. But it's rather like saying all women have the same size breasts. Size (as with breasts) is not the significant factor. The more important aspect is how love-making is carried out, with the man taking care to ensure he gives pleasure. Sometimes girls are frightened by the thought that they will not be able to accommodate a large penis. But remember that the vagina walls are elastic (they can stretch to allow the passage of a baby) and there is no question that 'it won't fit' (provided, that is, that your body is ready for sex).

Why do men orgasm easier/quicker than women?

At first sight doesn't it seem strange that God didn't make us identical in our enjoyment of pleasure? Why weren't we made to have simultaneous orgasms? But then perhaps such ease of experience would be unhelpful. Much of the joy of sexual discovery in marriage is the learning about the differences between the male and female sexual response. The husband needs to learn patience and to become sensitized to his wife's desires. The wife needs to express her feelings and discover how to prolong her husband's passion. The mutual fulfilment in coming together in sexual response is part of becoming one flesh just as much as the physical act of joining in sexual intercourse. Perhaps God wanted us to learn from each other and celebrate the differences He put in each one of us. We understand that true love is found not in our own pleasure, but is the overwhelming happiness of pleasing others.

If females know that men are turned on by what they see, why do they wear ski pants or bike shorts with no knickers on? Isn't that encouraging them to sin? This happens even in the church.

We've included this male-asked question because it involves you. Now it may be that he's saying, 'I can't help myself; it's not my fault', and so on — when he knows he should be keeping his lustful thoughts under better control. He has a responsibility too. But despite all that, there's still something for you as a girl to consider. It may be 'cool' to wear bike shorts with no underwear — we've heard it justified on the basis that 'I didn't want a panty line to show'. But having understood a little of the male sexual mind, is it helpful to act that way?

How do people who have been sexually active before joining the Church control their sexual desire?

Difficult question, this. For it is true that once you've experienced sexual activity, you can't just go

ME AND MY BODY

Thirty ways to describe how you look. Underline the way you see yourself as if you were looking at your body in the mirror. Be honest: don't be proud, and don't put yourself down either.

just right	**sexy**	**well-developed**
well-proportioned	**tall**	**ordinary**
too thin	**healthy**	**feeble**
small	**ugly**	**wonderful**
strong	**elegant**	**awkward**
average	**large**	**pleasant**
beautiful	**cute**	**appealing**
odd	**funny**	**repulsive**
attractive	**seductive**	**graceful**
too fat	**athletic**	**pretty**

Now think how important these descriptions will be when you're 60! While you need to believe in yourself, remember that the outward appearance is certainly not the most important thing. And your too-long nose or too-small breasts or too-fat tummy that you worry about so much will not worry the person who really does fall in love with you. For you as a person are more than the way your body looks.

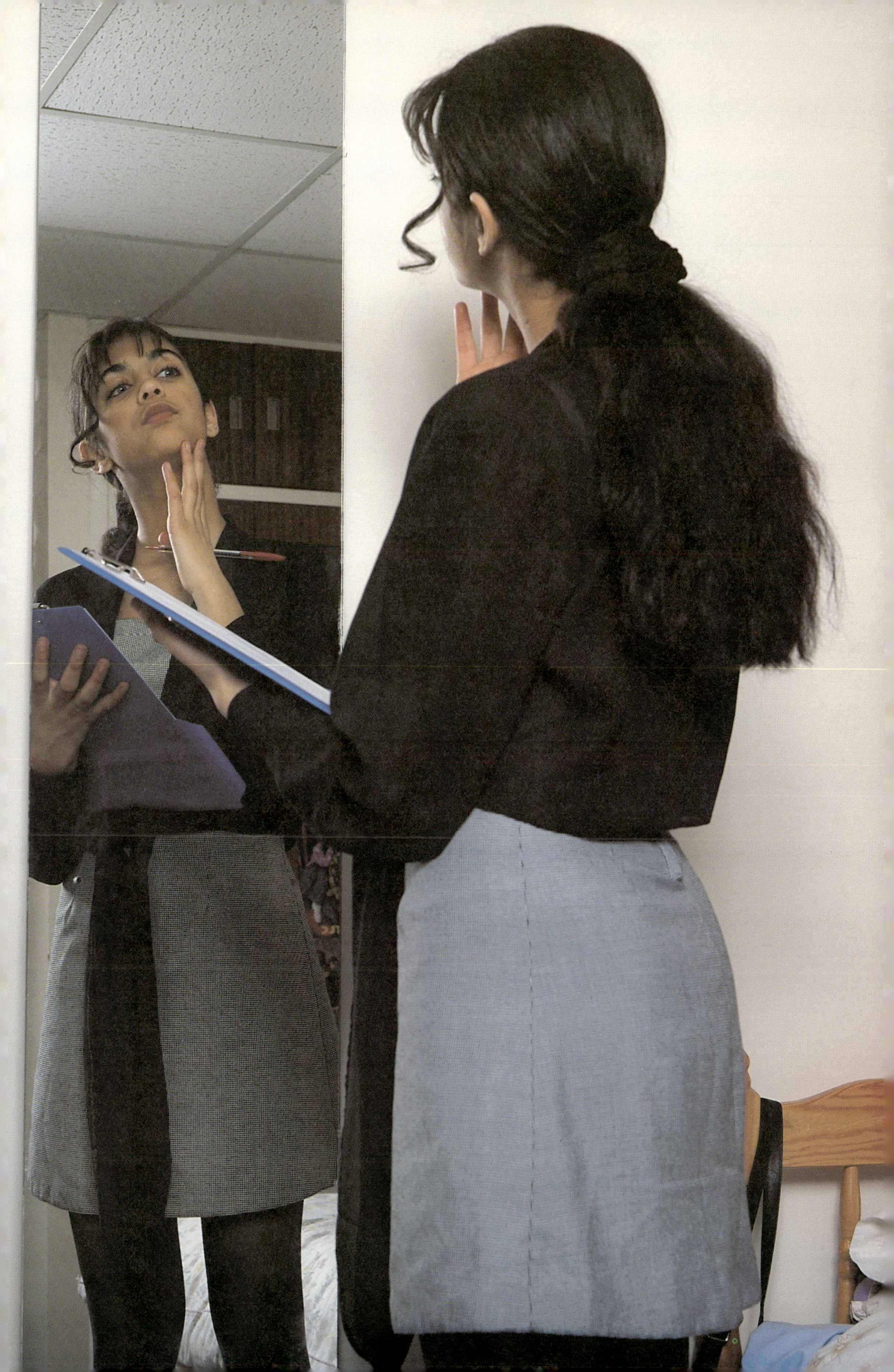

back and pretend it didn't happen. Your body has already become used to certain forms of stimulation, and suddenly to stop does cause real problems. Not least because you don't want to get so obsessed by sex that it affects your new Christian experience.

But neither do you want to continue harmful sexual activities. So it's a question of the same healing change that comes with conversion. You need to ask God to cure the damage of sin in your life in the sexual area as well as everywhere else. We're not saying this will prove easy and that temptations will not come along. But in the same way as you avoided circumstances and situations that might lead to problems before you had sex, then do the same now that you want to live a moral life. In just one aspect it may even be less difficult — at least you now know exactly what you are avoiding!

All teenagers are subject to intense media and peer pressure to conform to 'anything goes' behaviour. It sounds great, gives a quick thrill but doesn't give long-term satisfaction.

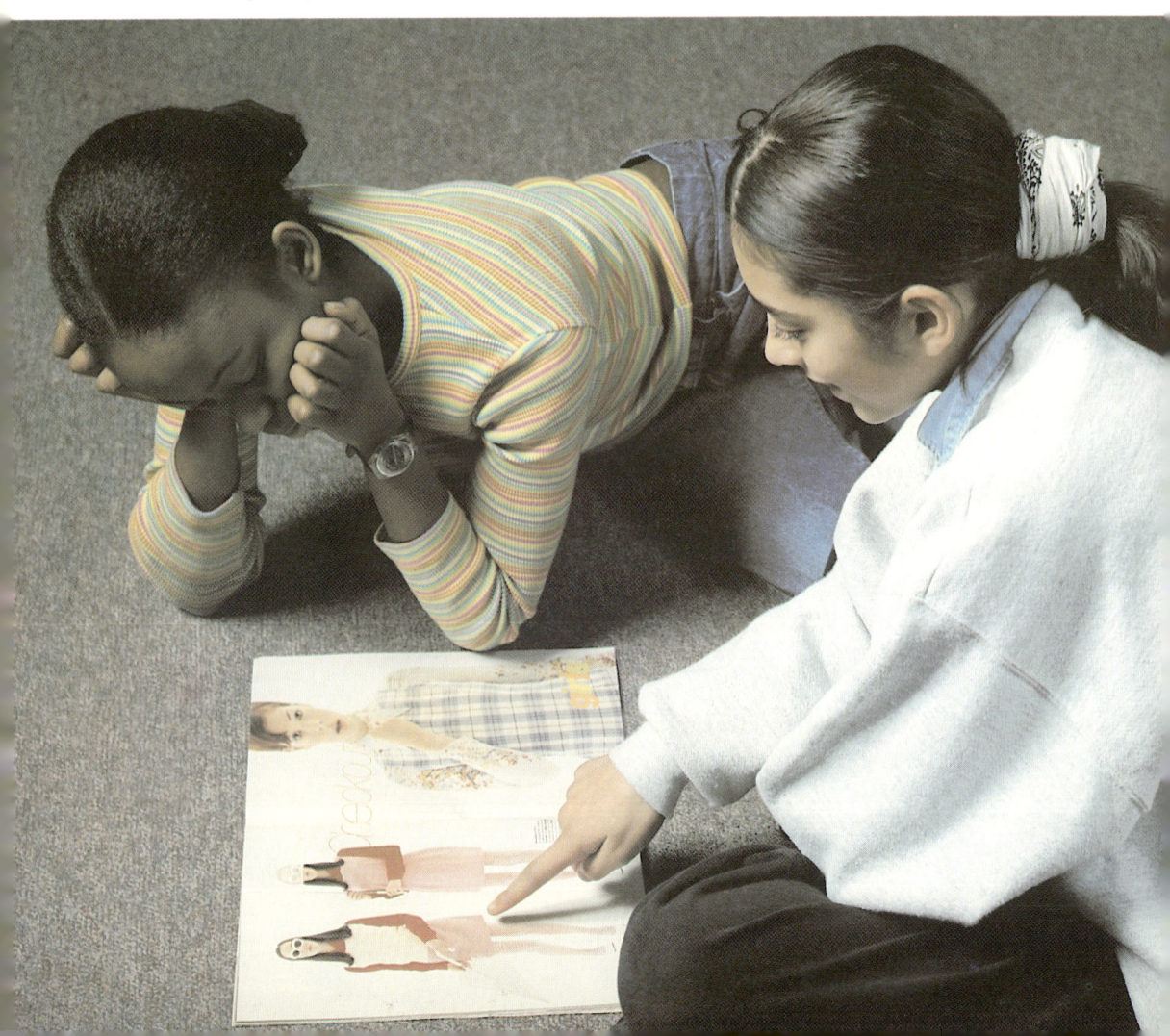

CASE STUDY

Here Susan puts into her own words how she felt about her sexual experience. See what you can learn from what she says:

'It started one warm and sunny afternoon when Brian picked me up and took me to the beach where we walked and talked till it got dark. Maybe it was because we could touch each other, or because we were both in our swimming costumes, but I began to get excited. I could see I was having the same kind of effect on Brian, and it made me feel good about myself.

'I noticed he was looking at me a bit different than usual, and kept on turning away. That's when I realized I was making him have an erection. It was a bit awkward, and I didn't want to seem to tempt him. But I felt flattered anyway.

'A couple of times when we were messing around he accidentally touched my breasts. That made me feel funny too, but it was kind of nice as well. When we arrived home, my family was out so we made ourselves comfortable. Brian sat down beside me and started stroking me, so gently. Then we kissed, and the kisses got longer and more passionate. We had the lights off so I couldn't see what he was doing, but I could feel it! I felt light-headed, and almost about to faint.

'Then Brian started hugging me close and moving his hands over my breasts. I noticed my nipples were sticking out more than usual. His touch was like an electric shock, and although I didn't want to get out of control I didn't want to stop either. As we pressed together I could feel his penis through his trousers. It was big and hard, and it seemed he wanted me to touch him there. He kept on having to adjust his position — maybe his erection made it uncomfortable for him.

'We both knew we were getting really involved, and stopped occasionally. But we were like magnets and kept on coming back to each other. So in the end we just let it happen, and we undressed each other and made love.

'Afterwards we both felt bad about going so far, but the damage had been done. So now we do it nearly every time we meet. We never seem to plan to, and we both agree it's not helping our relationship, but we can't keep our hands off each other. It seems once you start it's hard to stop.'

COMMENTS
Was it accidental that they excited each other?
Was it accidental that they sat alone in the house?
Was it accidental that they had the lights off?
Was it accidental that they spent a long time kissing?
Was it accidental that they kept on coming back to each other?
So in the end, was it accidental that they had sexual intercourse?
How would you advise them now?

4

This crazy little thing called love

Love comes from God. Whoever loves is a child of God and knows God. Whoever does not love does not know God . . . . 1 John 4:7, 8.

SO WHAT'S IT ALL ABOUT?

Though we've looked at some of the physical aspects of sex, it's so important to link this to the principle of love. That's usually the problem with sex manuals or medical textbooks. They leave out the higher reasons, the morals and the ethics which make us truly human.

You ask yourself: Why do questions about love and sex bother me anyway? Why is it so strange? What is this sexual mystery that people speak about?

And what of God? How is He involved in falling in love? Is it something God ignores?

This crazy little thing called love. Little? If people's actions are anything to go by, love is anything but little! One guy told us his story:

'I remember falling in love for the first time. She sat in front of me in the top class of the junior school. I would have been 10. Why was I so in love? Because she was brighter, cleverer and better at just about everything. Pure adoration. And when I eventually screwed up the courage to tell her I wanted to kiss her, she just said, "Yuk", and walked off.

'It was pain, agony for the next five minutes. Then the boys got me playing football and I forgot about it all.'

That's an easy story to tell. But the truth is that when love is so much more for real then the agony can seem forever. So what is love?

In today's world, 'love' is an abused word. Love is a second-hand emotion, according to one pop song. Another says that love is all you need. A third denies it exists at all.

Then there's a whole series of cartoons that begin 'Love is . . .' 'Love is never having to say you're sorry.' If you believe that, then you are really in trouble!

Is love like being sick, or mad, or both? Maybe if you are in love, or have been, that is what it felt like. As someone defined it, 'Love is a universal migraine'! Trouble is, if love is a disease, mental or otherwise, it implies that you need to be cured of it. And the doubters say that's what marriage does. But the *principle* of love is far more than infatuation and sick feelings. How tragic that the very idea that is used in the Bible to describe God is viewed as being ill.

How about this definition of love which is supposed to come from a psychiatrist:

'Love: the cognitive affective state characterized by intrusive and obsessive fantasizing concerning reciprocity of amorant feelings by the object of the amorance.'

Wow! That hardly helps either, does it?

Others have had higher ideas. Like Martin Luther, who said that love is, 'An image of God . . . the living essence of the divine nature which beams full of all goodness.' Or in the words of Emerson, love is, 'Our highest word, and the synonym of God.'

Remember: when you love, you reflect God. That's a powerful thought! So isn't it important to do it right?

(Maybe now would be a good time to take the 'Love Test'.)

MADE TO LOVE

We are made to love. Strange, isn't it? Do you remember that time when you were a kid, and boys were just a troublesome nuisance?

And now, well? What makes them tick?

You ask yourself: Why am I interested in the first place? What should I do about it? How should I behave?

Love definitions

Love makes the world go round. Love is all you need. What the world needs now is love, sweet love. A lot of talk about love — and a lot of nonsense too! A few definitions from poets, philosophers and the like . . . .

LOVE IS:
A kind of warfare.
OVID

A grave mental disease.
PLATO

A mutual misunderstanding.
OSCAR WILDE

A sickness full of woes, all remedies refusing.
SAMUEL DANIEL

Desperate madness.
JOHN FORD

Just another four-letter word.
TENNESSEE WILLIAMS

A kind of vaccination which saves a man from catching the complaint a second time.
HONORE DE BALZAC

A temporary insanity curable by marriage or by removal of the patient from the influences under which he incurred the disorder.
AMBROSE BIERCE

A beautiful dream with glandular activity.
EUGENE E. BRUSSELL

And then those more practical questions — will I know what to do? Will I be able to kiss properly? How can I practise?! (One girl confessed that the first time she kissed a boy she bit him!)

That first sudden kiss on the cheek that sent you into a spin.

To start with, let's try to understand what is happening here! What is love for me? How do I handle it? Why does it bother so many people?

Most of all it just gets so *personal*. Love makes us look at ourselves and see how we relate to others around us. That's perhaps why we get uncomfortable talking about feelings that are so close to home — especially when we can't explain why we feel why we do! But those tingly feelings, those shivers down the spine, those sideways glances are very real and need to be dealt with.

SEX AND LOVE

In the most recent survey of sex-

LOVE ACTIVITY

Look at the following ideas about love. Tick those you agree with, put a cross against those you disagree with:

☑ When another person's needs are as important as your own.
ABE BURROWS

☒ Two minds without a single thought.
PHILIP BARRY

☑ A grave mental disease.
PLATO

☑ The blinding revelation that some other being can be more important to the lover than he is to himself.
J. V. CASSERLEY

☑ To place our happiness in the happiness of another.
GOTTFRIED VON LEIBNITZ

☑ The effort a man makes to be satisfied with only one woman.
PAUL GERALDY

☑ To communicate to the other that you are all for him, that you will never fail him or let him down when he needs you, but that you will always be standing by with all the necessary encouragements.
ASHELY MONTAGUE

☒ A game in which both players always cheat.
EDGAR W. HOWE

☑ A mutual self-giving which ends in self-recovery.
FULTON J. SHEEN

☑ The more subtle form of self-interest.
HOLBROOK JACKSON

☒ Sentimental measles.
CHARLES KINGSLEY

☑ Love means that the attributes of the lover are changed into those of the Beloved.
JUNAYD OF BAGHDAD

ual attitudes in the UK, the most common reason women gave for their first experience of sexual intercourse was 'being in love'. For men this answer came third, after 'curiosity' and 'natural follow on.'

It really is important to know what being in love really means. Why? Because many who think they are in love and have sex find that all is not rosy a little further down the romantic road. In that same survey more than one in four women felt that they had sex too early. Many girls have told us, 'I gave in too easily', or, 'I was pressured into it', or, 'Since I thought I was in love I felt I had to do it.'

You may think you're in love. How do you know? If you find yourself really *liking* a boy, you just try and write down *why!* Hard, isn't it?

Writing all this down may make it seem rather cold and calculating. But at least it tells you that looks aren't everything. Especially when you think that people's looks change (sometimes a whole lot!) during their lives, and marriage is meant to be a lifetime commitment. Love based on looks may not last long.

Now you may not be that much closer to saying exactly *why* you may love someone. But would you really want to *stay* in love with someone you honestly disliked?! Character is far more important in the long run.

HOW TO CHOOSE?

You would hardly want to follow

WHY DO I LIKE HIM?

Try this out. Look at the list below. Circle some of the qualities that appeal to you. Then go back through and see which ones apply to someone you like. At least then you may have something to work on:

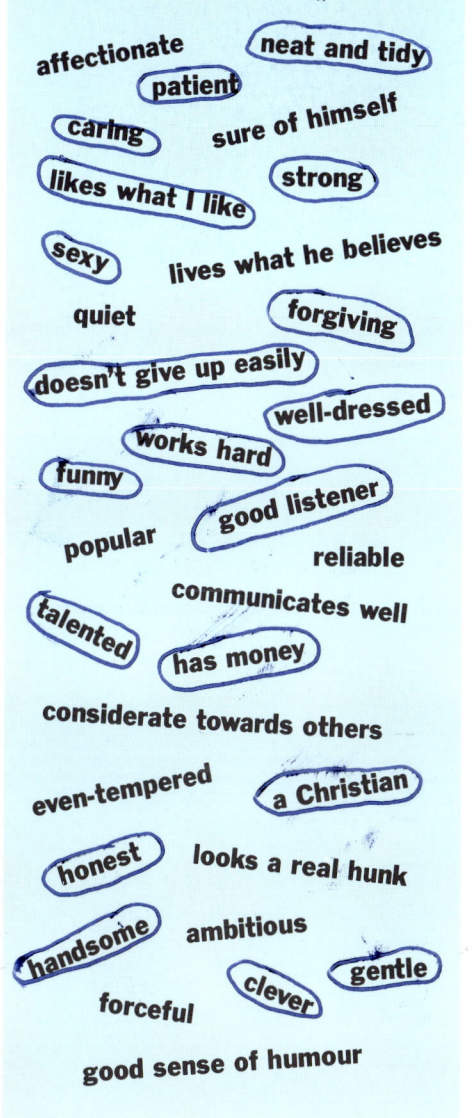

affectionate
neat and tidy
patient
caring
sure of himself
likes what I like
strong
sexy
lives what he believes
quiet
forgiving
doesn't give up easily
well-dressed
works hard
funny
good listener
popular
reliable
communicates well
talented
has money
considerate towards others
even-tempered
a Christian
honest
looks a real hunk
handsome
ambitious
clever
gentle
forceful
good sense of humour

the method of a student we knew. He wanted to be married before he left college, so he drew up a list of eligible girls, and went around proposing until he got 'Yes' for an answer! Whether he prioritized the list, and how far down the list he got we don't know!

You can't make yourself fall in love, nor can you make someone else fall in love with you. The very essence of love is mutual attraction, but despite what people say, love cannot be blind.

We remember counselling a family with three teenage girls. We spoke with them and gave them some material on choosing a partner, Christian marriage and so on.

'But,' they said, 'we're not thinking about getting married. We don't even have boy-friends. So why give us this stuff now?'

'Because by the time you decide it'll be too late,' we replied.

All too often couples come to see us and ask for premarital counselling after they've made their minds up on just about everything. Then it's the hardest thing in the world to suggest that they may not be very compatible.

And even the most compatible of partners can break up. Why? Often it's because they can't agree on the basics of life. You may come from the same country, even the same town; have similar social backgrounds, even like the same foods. But if the *direction* is not the same,

GOING OUT TOGETHER

A Yes/No quiz for you on the Who, the What and the When of getting friendly.

YES NO I would always check with my parents before going out with a boy.

YES NO I prefer to go out as a group rather than just the two of us.

YES **NO** I like to kiss the first time I go somewhere with a boy.

YES NO If I get too serious, I stop!

YES NO I make it very clear to the boy when he's going too far.

YES NO I try to avoid getting into difficult situations.

YES NO I like to do something other than kiss and cuddle when I go with someone.

YES NO I want to know beforehand where we're going.

YES NO I'm careful not to dress too temptingly.

YES NO I always make sure I get home at a reasonable time.

CHOICES

How do I choose?

Try to write out what areas are important to you in making your choice.

How are you going to make your mind up?

What is important to you?

---

then it will all unravel. That's why the Bible asks, 'Can two walk together, except they be agreed?' (Amos 3:3, KJV.) That's *not* saying that you have to agree on everything — but you do have to agree which way you're going. Or as one mother told her headstrong daughter about to marry a similarly-minded boy, 'If you join two battle tanks together, they'd better be pulling in the same direction!'

Then there's the whole question of allowing others to make your decisions for you: either by indirect control of who you go out with, or through actual arranging of the marriage itself. All these situations have their own problems. If your parents are trying to marry you to someone you truly dislike, then that can be a recipe for disaster. Forced marriage strikes at the heart of God's intention of mutual love and honour. But neither is following your own heart alone necessarily a good way either. Whatever the customs of your society, always remember that the Bible comes before

Unless you can agree on the direction your lives should go even though you have many similarities in character, likes and dislikes, it could all fall apart.

anything else. Make sure your ideas about love and marriage come from God, and not from Hollywood or your local society.

So if you are involved, what direction are you both going? To us that's the real question. And we're not necessarily talking about where you're going to live, what careers you're going to have, or even the way you think.

If you both share a trust in God, can pray and discuss together, you have a formula for a sincere and rewarding relationship.

THE FUNDAMENTALS

The questions we would like you to ask yourself are:

What is most important to me? What does life mean to me? Where will I spend eternity? REAL questions of life and death, of God and your eternal destiny.

If you and your future husband can agree on these ideals, these objectives, the fundamentals of faith in God, then you can deal with all the other problems and differences. But if the *basics* of life and its meaning are not agreed, then whatever else you have in common may not be enough to keep you together. That's not to say there's a magic Christian formula that guarantees success (there are enough Christians getting divorced to disprove that theory). But when the foundation is built together with God it is far more secure.

So while there are never any certainties in the success or failure of human relationships, having the God of Love at the heart of love is surely the best answer. How do we know? Because He's been there at the centre of our marriage for the past twenty years; and so we love more, better, and deeper now than the day we married.

QUESTIONS AND ANSWERS

Do you believe that love at first sight occurs between Christians?

Sometimes the term 'love at first sight' has some kind of magical idea about it, as if you don't have any choice but to fall in love. It may be true that you don't consciously choose who you are attracted to, but that doesn't mean you *have* to act on that attraction. Many couples have told us of instant attraction when they met. Sadly this 'love at first sight' is no more a guarantee of a successful relationship than love that develops slowly. It is sometimes a hindrance to looking at your partner objectively. So yes, we do believe in an immediate attraction between Christians, but we would hesitate to call it love — because love is not just a feeling, but a fundamental principle of life. Looking back, you may believe it was love at first sight, but more realistically your current love has been transferred backwards to those initial feelings of attraction.

Is it wrong to marry someone I don't love and feel I will never love, but because I feel that no one else will come into my life I will go along with it? I find my future partner to be totally unattractive and demanding and a bit ignorant. But at the same time he can be fun to be with.

While there are examples of couples falling in love *after* they've married, they are definitely the exception. We would counsel you to think very seriously about going ahead with a marriage on these terms. Certainly you should seek some good advice, for even though he may be fun to be with your assessment that he is 'totally unattractive, demanding and a bit ignorant', and you believe you can never love him, means that you have already decided negatively. Perhaps you are older and think this is your only chance. Perhaps there are other reasons why you would wish to marry him. But without something far more definite in its favour we could not recommend marriage on these terms.

Do you think it is wrong to go out with a non-Christian?

So often we want to know why you asked the question! Of course it is not *wrong* to go out with a non-Christian. However, by asking the question you show that you realize there are potential problems. The basics of good behaviour should of course be the same whoever he is, Christian or not. But you do have the right to expect the Christian to operate from higher moral principles. (That some who call themselves Christian break these principles does not remove the expectation.)

Association with non-Christians is not wrong. Jesus associated with those who were looked down on as ungodly in his society. But it would be foolish to ignore the possible problems of greater pressure for a

Expressing your love in a letter can mean giving exaggerated compliments that you might be embarrassed to say face to face. But then that's why they're written!

sexual relationship, of different expectations, or of the use of tactics that a Christian might not use.

Behind your question is perhaps this thought: 'If you believe you should not marry a non-Christian, why should you even bother to date one?' If you are strong in your faith you can show what it really means to be a Christian. You may even be able to influence him for good. Be careful, however, that he is not merely doing things just to please you! As in all relationships, you need to be very objective as to what is happening, and what your mutual expectations are. And remember that if he cannot accept your fundamental beliefs about God, then any long-term relationship or marriage will be difficult because you are going in different directions.

What is a real love letter? Should it have God in its message?

A real love letter? You have to ask?! Mind you, it is not always easy to tell what is really true in love letters. Sometimes people write what they think the other wants to read, not what they really mean. But you would have to work that out by asking directly.

The business about involving God is more interesting. A love letter that quoted texts every other line might be viewed as an exercise in what someone once called 'pretentious piety'! On the other hand, a love relationship between Christians that never gets to talking about God is in deep trouble. You need to think about the way you express yourself intimately: Am I embarrassed to mention God when I declare my love? Why is that? Do I see God as Someone who would interfere? Is He like a policeman ready to stop me when I break the rules? Or is He like a referee who is going to call 'foul' when He thinks I've gone too far? If God is a natural Friend to you, this will come over automatically in your friendship with your boy-friend.

Is it right to keep my boy-friend secret from my parents?

Much is behind this question. We would like to know more of the

Only if in some way you are ashamed of your boy-friend should you worry about your parents finding out about your relationship.

reasons. Is the expectation that your parents will disapprove, and you may even half-agree with them? Is it because in some way you are ashamed of your boy-friend? Why? Is it just because of the way he dresses, or is it his behaviour? Parents object for many reasons, especially protective fathers! However, if you know your parents want the best for you, and are not critical just to be awkward, then you should not try to keep a boy-friend a secret from them. Think what may happen if they find out accidentally. What will this do to your relationship with them? They may feel that you don't trust them and their judgement.

And then what will your boy-friend think? That you're embarrassed about him? Or that you mistrust your parents/don't like them/are scared of them? While you may not wish to discuss every aspect of your relationships with your parents, and you may not want to bring every boy you like home, if you are serious about someone, he needs to meet your family and vice versa.

Every girl needs reassurance that she is special and appreciated.

Why is it that my boy-friends never compliment me?

Really? If your current boy-friend never compliments you, find one who does! We're not talking about flattery here, but we all need to have positive reassurance. Love needs to be made more specific: 'I like the way you do this . . . .' 'I appreciate that you think that . . . .' Even, 'I love the way you do your hair.' If your boy-friend cannot be bothered to compliment you for anything, he's just not worth the trouble.

Mind you, do you ever compliment him?

Do you think that 14 is too young to date guys? Or do you think it's OK so long as you do not get too involved with them?

The right age to date cannot be made into some general answer. Like much in relationships, it depends. It depends on the situation, the culture, and what exactly is being proposed. For 14-year-olds to be out all night or to be running around who knows where is certainly out of order. But to begin relating to boys, especially in a group, is helpful for the development of good, healthy relationships later. So the answer is that it depends on what a date is, and you should be able to decide what is appropriate or not. Certainly any situation where sexual intercourse is possible has to be totally avoided — even the secular law defines this as criminal activity.

LOVE TEST

- Love wants to give.
  Lust wants to take.
  What do you want?

- Love means you also like.
  Do you really like each other?

- What about God?
  Is He involved in your relationship?

- Are you good friends as well as everything else?

- Do you trust each other — even with your most intimate secrets?

- Love is unselfish.
  Lust is selfish.
  What are you?

- Are you able to laugh and share fun together?

- When you have fights, can you work out your differences?

- Can you talk about everything and anything together?

- Are you *both* in love — not just one of you?

- Love is wise.
  Infatuation is foolish.
  Which are you?

- Do you believe your relationship will last?

What has love got to do with sex?

For some, very little; for most, quite a lot! You must understand that there is a progression in physical affections that leads eventually to sexual intercourse. Our bodies are made that way. Sex is a normal part of that love which exists between a man and a woman, and should therefore be part of marriage. Sometimes in today's world, sex is divorced from love, and made to be something on its own. Sex can never be meaningful like that. Sex may be part of love, but not the other way around.

You can express your love in ways without sex, and before marriage this is what should happen. But as most couples know, the drive towards a sexual relationship is very strong, and if not handled correctly, can even destroy true love. Think of sex as God's great way of showing physical love, and follow His guidance in its use!

Do you think it is wise for me to stay out late with my boy-friend if we are alone and have different morals?

You already know the answer to that one. You're just looking for reassurance that your position is the right one. If you don't think it's wise, don't do it!

5

Sex and the modern world

Don't let the world around you squeeze you into its own mould, but let God re-mould your minds from within. Romans 12:2, Phillips.

THE WORLD AS IT IS

'Sex is,' said Gore Vidal. And so it *is*. In this modern world, it is everywhere. You'd have to live in a convent not to believe otherwise. And maybe even there you'd not be safe from today's ideas about sex.

We once read a story about a nun who, after a number of years, left her convent and returned to life outside. What hit her hardest were:

▸ the revealing fashions
▸ the nudity on TV
▸ the sexual overtones in conversation
▸ the use of sexual images in advertising
▸ the acceptance of immorality in magazines and books

For someone who had lived such a sheltered existence, the modern emphasis on sex was a great shock.

And maybe if you thought about it, the stress on sex would shock you too. The trouble is that most of us have got used to it. Semi-nude pictures in national papers. Immorality is normal in movies, plays, books. Divorce is commonplace. If you don't sleep with your boy-friend, you're odd. If it feels good, says your favourite magazine, DO IT! Illegitimate babies are normal for teenagers in many places today. Adultery is hardly seen as wrong. Morality fades away as people just think of themselves.

As the British newspaper the *Independent on Sunday* (16 January 1994) admitted: 'Sex dominates the late twentieth-century media — newspaper reports, films, television series, modern novels and advertisements all present powerful ideas and confusing images of what is acceptable and what is desirable.' Wherever you look, the smiling face of illicit sex leers at you.

EVERYBODY'S DOING IT

OK, so it's there. The real question is, what do you do about it? The urge to conform is very powerful, but rarely acknowledged. Much of what we do is because of everybody else. In the words of the song, 'Everybody's doing it', and so we do too. Like sheep we follow right along.

So what are the facts? These are from the UK: 'Acceptance of sex before marriage is now nearly universal. Only 8.2 per cent of men and 10.8 per cent of women believed it to be always or mostly wrong.' (*The Sunday Review*, 16 January 1994, page 8.)

In this report on sexual activity in Britain (with a total of 18,876 people interviewed), the general acceptance of premarital sex is spelled out. Three quarters of the population saw nothing wrong in it. How the nation's morals have changed, when only 5 per cent of men and 4 per cent of women who experienced sex before marriage thought they had done anything wrong. And among the young only 1 in 20 in the age group 16-24 believed premarital sex was wrong. The survey concludes: 'First sex within marriage is now almost unknown.' (page 6.)*

Ask yourself, what do these questions have as their essence:

▶ What am I, the last virgin?
▶ Come on, can't you see what the rest are doing?

Sex is the dominant force in much of the media aimed at the teenager. If you don't take part you're freaky. After all it's free, it's fun and it's the hottest thing around — so they say!

To make personal decisions that contradict the ideas of your peers may mean being looked upon as odd or out of touch.

▸ All my friends are doing it. Why not me?
▸ Do you think I can't find someone who will?
▸ Why deny myself something everyone else is enjoying?

Do you see the hidden agenda, the unspoken assumptions? If you don't, or won't, then you are:

> ☐ odd
> ☐ not part of the crowd
> ☐ out of touch with reality
> ☐ not like others
> ☐ different from everybody else
> ☐ and most significantly —
>   *not my friend*.

That kind of pressure is hard to fight. We all look around for reassurance. We want to be told that what we're doing is being accepted. We look for the comfort of our friends, the group we are with. Trouble is that this means that our thoughts and behaviour are being controlled by others — and in ways that may eventually hurt us.

Is that what you would really want to do? Have sex because everybody else says they are having sex?

So many girls have said that their first sexual experiences were due to a need for acceptance, to do 'the right thing'. Sadly, in trying to do the right thing they did the wrong thing.

From then on, it's easy to think that a mistake with one sexual partner can be solved by finding another. Many young people have fallen into this trap, desperately searching for the partner who matches what they are looking for, the one who can fill that aching void they feel inside. To quote the survey again: 'It is also notable that the earlier sexual activity starts the greater the likelihood of multiple partners.' (page 7.) The survey also shows that on average, well over 60 per cent of both men and women have had more than one sexual partner. As Sydney J. Harris puts it: 'Grandmother called it a "sin"; mother called it an "affair"; daughter calls it an "experience."' How attitudes have changed — for the worse.

MODERN SEX MYTHS

Added to the pressure to conform and the 'It's not a sin anymore' ideas are the modern sex myths. Myths are stories that some people believe but which are not true. Let's look at a few examples of the modern world's glamorous presentation of sex.

'SEX IS JUST SO INCREDIBLE'
Yes, it may well be — especially when you know it's right! But many people, both male and female, have told us of their disappointments in sex. 'It was nothing like I expected. I didn't feel the earth move, or have fireworks going off inside my head. In fact it was shabby and rather ugly.' Someone else told us, 'Afterwards I said to myself, "Was that

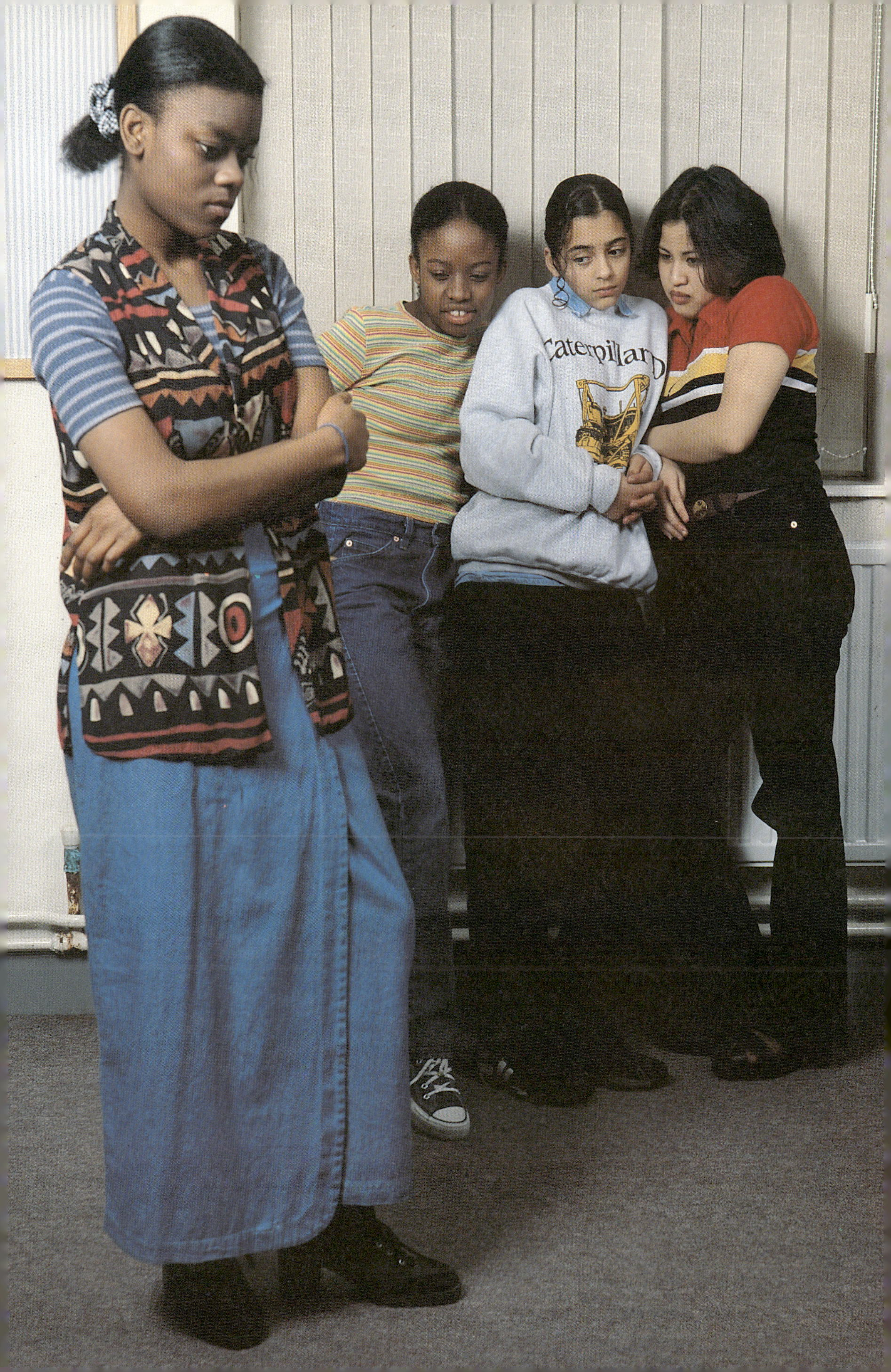
Caterpillar

it?" I certainly didn't find it something to rave about, and I wondered whether it was me.' To have an amazingly exciting first sexual experience is certainly a rarity, and almost impossible behind the bike shed. The best sexual experiences are between couples who know each other very well, have complete trust in one another, and have built up a shared relationship of which sex is just a part.

'SLEEPING AROUND IS FUN'

Often said, but we doubt it is really experienced, except by those for whom sex is a drug to ease the pain of something else. What the myth does not tell you is the agony of doubt, the terrible sense of guilt, the fear of betrayal. In pornography, sex is just fun, fun, fun. In real life, such actions are rarely guiltless. Fantasy is one thing, but the harsh reality of those brief moments of sex is all too often a lifetime of remorse and shame. Men and women live a lifetime desperately searching for self-forgiveness. We know. We've seen it.

'SEX DOESN'T HURT YOU'

Lay back and enjoy it, says the myth. Please yourself, and don't worry. Tell that to all the pregnant 14-year-olds, the aborted babies, those infected with genital warts and gonorrhoea and syphilis and AIDS, those with tortured consciences and broken lives. Wrong sex is not a victimless crime as all the wreckage of modern society shows all too graphically.

'SEX IS NECESSARY TO BE A REAL PERSON'

This myth comes in more subtly. You know the argument from the sex seller: 'You're not a real woman unless you've had sex. It's part of growing up. It's what adults do. You're a big girl now.' The idea is that like having periods and buying bras, sex is a normal part of growing older and more mature. What this myth doesn't tell you is that mature people aren't so easily fooled!

'SEX IS ESSENTIAL IN A RELATIONSHIP'

Like the previous myth, this myth is another clever perversion of the truth. It hides under the need for intimacy, it says that you must show your depth of feeling through sex. You know the line, 'If you really loved me, you would . . . .' By taking true feelings of love and care, this myth exploits them and turns them inside out. Those who use this myth make demands that never should be made.

'SEX IS JUST PHYSICAL'

The emphasis on the feelings and senses in this myth means that the mental and spiritual bonding is left out. How can you take part in sex and keep it 'just as a physical thing' so that it doesn't interfere with other aspects of your life? This is such a degradation of God's gift! If sex is just physical, the joining of genitals,

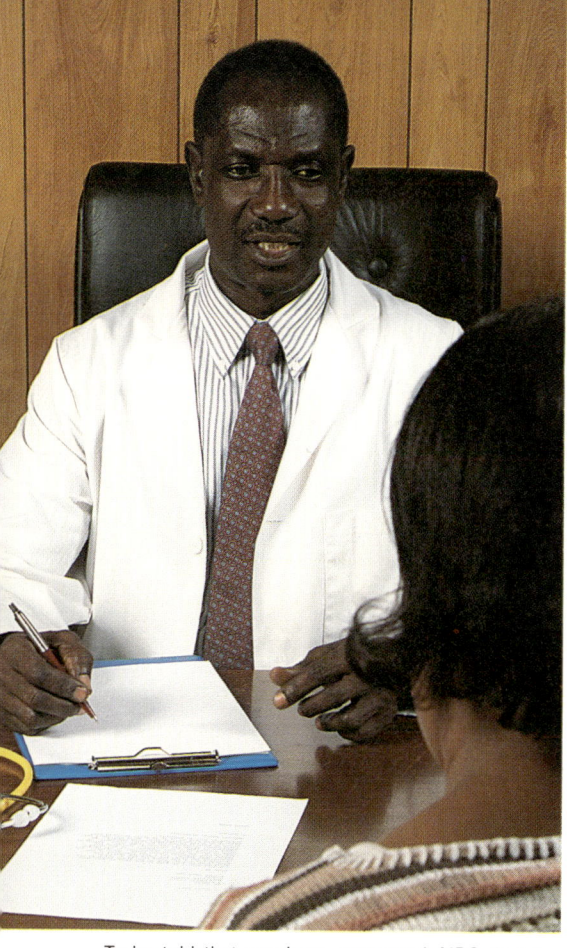

To be told that you have contracted AIDS destroys your world. The promiscuous, homosexuals and drug addicts are those most at risk.

then it is reduced to the level of responding to a biological urge. That hardly makes sex look so wonderful — if it is just a part of something we *have* to do, like eating or breathing.

'SEX IS NOBODY ELSE'S BUSINESS EXCEPT YOURS'

If this myth is true, why are there more than 250 million cases of sexually-transmitted diseases reported worldwide each year? AIDS, abortion, rape, incest, divorce statistics make sex everybody's business — especially when you recognize the uncounted cost of wrong sex in society. Sex with your current partner affects your next partner and so on — not just in terms of communicable diseases but in emotional damage and feelings of guilt.

How hard we found it, listening to a girl asking what to tell her fiancé about her previous sexual experiences. What would you have advised?

Sex is meant to be private and intimate. You don't *want* to make it anybody else's business. But if that's really true, then you cannot sleep around! While it's your body, and you must choose how to use it, don't sell yourself short. Don't be fooled by the myths, and remember that each of us have a responsibility not only to ourselves, but to those around us and to God.

'SEX MAKES EVERYTHING ALL RIGHT'

If you are not sexually active, that's the reason for all your problems. You're hung-up, you're frustrated, you're repressing your natural desires. Just hop into bed and it'll all be OK! It will:

save you from loneliness
be emotionally fulfilling
cure your depression
increase your self-worth
make you successful at work

and so on. An amazing list of lies! These claims are as realistic as the false doctors selling fake remedies that will 'cure all your diseases'!

THE ANTIDOTE

Enough of the myths! What is the antidote, the cure? How do you stand against all the wrong ideas about sex?

'Do not conform yourselves to the standards of this world, but let God transform you inwardly by a complete change of your mind.' (Romans 12:2.)

There's so much in that powerful piece of advice! Don't conform — at least not in the area of today's sexual standards. Don't fall for this world's peer pressure, but be strong in following God's good advice. You don't have to follow what others tell you.

Be transformed by God. We all need the healing change that only He can provide. We have all believed wrong ideas about sex, and we need to be healed from our incorrect thinking.

Because what we need is *a complete change of mind.* A completely new way of understanding God's gift of sexuality, and seeing it as God sees it. Sex is not negative or sinful or wrong — not when God made sex. God gave us sex as a positive, loving, caring present from Him, a gracious Creator. Interesting, isn't it: today's phrase isn't about making love but having sex! Having it — in the same way as we say 'I just had lunch.'

The Bible is very clear in describing the kind of sinful people we are: 'What human nature does is quite plain. It shows itself in immoral, filthy and indecent actions.' (Galatians 5:19.)

As so many couples have found through bitter experience, you cannot find fulfilment when sex happens in something other than a relationship of total commitment and trust. Even the leaders of the sexual revolution are having second thoughts. Unlimited, irresponsible sex is not as good as they used to teach.

Maybe we can all begin to see why 'God wants you to be holy and completely free from sexual immorality' (1 Thessalonians 4:3). It's not because God wants to deny you pleasure. It's not because God has a down on things physical. It's not even because God is trying to stop you from showing your great love to someone else. It's because God so much wants it to be perfect for you — at least the best it can possibly be, finding ecstasy, joy and fulfilment in the arms of your life-long husband. Paul goes on with some words for the men — but they apply to you too: 'Each of you men should know how to live with his wife in a holy and honourable way, not with lustful desire, like the heathen who do not know God.' (1 Thessalonians 4:4.)

Why does he link lustful desire with those who don't know God? Could it be that denial or ignorance of God leads us to live just

The general message is, life-long relationships are not on, boring even, but God wants you to experience real joy and fulfilment with someone not for a quick thrill but for life.

biological lives? Just doing what comes naturally and not thinking of moral principles and higher spiritual things? Enough to make you think.

Some more counsel: 'Do not give in to bodily passions, which are always at war against the soul.' (1 Peter 2:11.) Sometimes excuses are made: 'I couldn't help myself. My body just took over. I didn't know what I was doing.'

Our answer to that is that if you know about your bodily passions (and notice the Bible doesn't say that to have them is *wrong*), then you can take care to avoid arousing situations and to walk out when those passions start building.

While the sexual chemistry is certainly strong, to give in is a defeat for 'the soul' — your spirituality. And it's not just 'inherited guilt' that causes you pain when as a Christian you sleep with your boyfriend. It's the damaging of your spiritual character, the hurt that you do to your relationship with God. Not just because He's saying, 'Don't do it — it's wrong!' but because you are walking away from God and

When you're aware of emotions getting out of control, call a break. Otherwise you can slide into situations which as a Christian you'll regret.

doing your own thing. Forbidden sex is self-destructive, not a punishment from an offended God.

'Avoid immorality. . . . Don't you know that your body is the temple of the Holy Spirit, who lives in you and who was given to you by God? You do not belong to yourselves but to God.' (1 Corinthians 6:18, 19.) That's the key: because you're a Christian, God is part of you. Look again at John 17:21-23, where Jesus prays for that unity between Himself, God and His followers, 'I in them and you in me.'

That's the kind of union that God is looking for. It's no accident that sex is also a union of two beings. So for God to be part of such a union, it must be one that is uplifting and not degrading, spiritual rather than animalistic, dignifying rather than demeaning.

The tragedy of our time is that we have taken God's exquisite gift of pleasure-giving and made it just the joining of bodies. Making sex equal to the physical reduces it to just one part. One dimension instead of the three dimensions: physical, mental and spiritual.

DIFFERENT WAYS OF LIVING

We're talking about two different ways of living, of two different ways of believing. In our modern world it's as if people have taken sex and tried to turn it into some kind of god. Sex is THE thing — and as we saw before, it is seen as a cure-all for your problems, and as such something almost worshipped. Maybe that's why Malcolm Muggeridge called sex, 'The ersatz or substitute religion of the twentieth

SEX: SO WHO'S TELLING THE TRUTH?

This multiple choice questionnaire is to help you see the great difference between the attitudes of modern society and Christian values. You need to decide who's telling the truth!

Sex before marriage is OK
When it's done in secret
Whenever
If you feel like it
Never
If you're in love

You feel tempted to have sex so you
Give in
See how long you can stand the temptation
Take a cold shower
Pray about it
Run as far from the temptation as possible

If you hear a sexual joke, do you
Laugh loudly
Look the other way
Tell one too
Leave the conversation
Tell them it's disgusting

Sexual sin is wrong because
There's no such thing as sexual sin
You might get pregnant
God says so
You can damage yourself emotionally and spiritually
You can get AIDS

Sex is supposed to be enjoyed
By anyone
Only if you're married
Even if you're just engaged
If you and your boy-friend want to
Sex is not supposed to be enjoyed

---

century.' Sex is not new, but the attention we pay to it and the way it is revered today has made sex into a kind of religion.

But this view of sex is a religion that has a rotten core. The way it is portrayed, sex is doing *your* thing, of experiencing *your* pleasure, of satisfying *your* desire, however way-out that may be. Today's description of sex is selfishness, which is at the heart of sin. The devil has turned sex from something you give into something you take. And in the end, none of this sexual idolatry satisfies the needs of an aching heart.

Instead of being a glamorized, guiltless, spiritual experience, this kind of sex is nothing more than an addiction to physical highs which, like drugs, leave you in a worse state than before. All the glittering night-time attraction fades in the harsh grey light of a despairing dawn.

LIVING FOOLISHLY

Miriam, a girl from a Christian home, gave up her principles so she

A popular but desperate way to escape emotional probems and pain.

could 'have fun'. She thought that what she was taught at church stopped her from enjoying herself. So as soon as she could, she stopped coming to church and went out with her friends — to have fun.

Now there's nothing wrong in having fun — as long as it's the right kind of fun. But Miriam thought that fun was found in drinking and drugs and the free sex she had at parties. Of course, she soon found out that sex is never free — in fact it can come with a high price tag.

Soon she was living with her boy-friend, who used to control her and hit her if she disobeyed. She was too frightened to leave, and life didn't seem so much fun anymore. So she started drinking more, as if the drink would help her to escape. Her boy-friend became more abusive, calling her a drunk, and forced her into unnatural sex.

Miriam used alcohol and drugs to ease her physical and emotional pain. In the end she was so low she was hardly living any more. And it certainly wasn't fun any more.

The Devil knows how to tempt and he knows how to hurt and destroy. The bright lights of parties, the excitement of sex, the trap of drink and drugs can end in disaster for your life.

Fun is not found in living foolishly. Losing control to any of these powerful temptations can destroy you. We want to tell you: a life with God is truly much more fun than any of these. 'Don't let the world around you squeeze you into its own mould, but let God re-mould your minds from within.' Romans 12:2, Phillips.

---

*There are recent studies which show that although adolescents often claim to be, or act as though they are, sexually active, in fact far fewer have had sex than is suggested in some newspaper surveys. Medical Editor.

QUESTIONS AND ANSWERS

Would you say that most marital problems are caused by sexual difficulties?

Sexual difficulties are often associated with problems in a marriage. But that is not to say they are necessarily *caused* by them. Sometimes they are the result of other problems, which then makes the whole situation worse. In the context of our current subject — sex in the modern world — we believe that the unhealthy over-emphasis on selfish sexual fulfilment does contribute to relationship problems. Each partner has been told what to expect, and when things don't work as they want, they start blaming each other. So it's really important to be aware *now*, before you marry, that the ideas you may have been taught about sex are not necessarily right. Look again at the sex myths discussed earlier. Have you believed some of these? And then see what God is saying, and what the truth is!

Far from saving a relationship, an over-emphasis on selfish sex can put further pressure on a couple with problems.

Is it wrong for a Christian woman to have silicone injected in order to enlarge her breasts?

Another question that reflects the modern preoccupation with looks, which is linked with sexual attractiveness. (In this answer we're ignoring any reconstructive surgery that may be necessary after a mastectomy [removal of part or all of the breast].) The main reason for this procedure is to increase breast size, which is seen as desirable for a fuller figure. The idea is that in this way you will increase your attractiveness to men.

This leads into the whole area of improving on nature, which ranges from light makeup to full surgical remodelling. Some who want to take the option of breast enlargement are doing so because of the false perspectives on sex we've mentioned. That's not to say we do not make ourselves as presentable as we can — to say we should do nothing because 'that's the way God made us' would leave a very hairy, smelly mass of humanity! But to undertake surgery is a different matter and, because of the current concerns over the safety of breast implants, we would generally advise against.

Why are men so affected by looking at women?

The easy answer is to say, 'That's the way they're programmed.' You maybe have wondered why men react so differently to you. You just dressed nicely, and some guy took it to mean you were available or something. It's important to recognize the difference in the sexes, especially in the area of visual stimulation. Of course, men must not excuse their lustful looks, and you should be aware that you do not want to cause any problems either. Instead of trying to blame one another, it would be good to admit people but as objects. That is a particularly male temptation we'll mention again, but it is linked to the modern over-emphasis on the glamorization and corruption of sex.

How should a Christian live in a sex-mad world?

Firstly, as we've said, realize the situation. (That doesn't mean you have to explore everything, either!) Recognize that there are great differences in the way modern society thinks and behaves, and the way God has advised. Then make sure you have the antidote — spending time studying the Bible, praying about your concerns, and understanding God's better way. Thirdly, put sex in its place. It is not *everything*, and many people live good, fulfilled and happy lives without sex. You need to have the right perspective on sex as a talent that, properly used, can be of mutual benefit to your husband and yourself.

Are the new sex clinics right for Christians?

This question asked by a teenager seems to be getting ahead of the subject — since these sex clinics are generally for those having sexual problems in marriage/living together. But it's important to think what kind of philosophy is behind these institutions. Is it Christian? Are they concerned with spiritual matters? Or is it a question of dealing with physical problems? Of course, many problems are in the mind anyway, to do with the way we see things, and the clinics deal with these too. But

that men like looking and women like displaying, and this is OK since it is part of God's way of bringing us together through mutual attraction. The problem is when our selfish thoughts become involved and we treat each other not as what about some of the treatments that certain sex practitioners suggest — of substitute lovers and group activities? Once again the problem of different sexual values in today's world could prove difficult to the Christian.

We would be far more comfortable with Christians who have sexual problems seeking help from a Christian counsellor or family doctor. Sometimes supposed professionals have told a Christian client that their difficulties are due to 'outdated sexual taboos' or 'guilt associated with religion'. Their advice has been to 'give up on this old-fashioned religious stuff and enjoy yourself'. Not only is this unprofessional, but such advice could well cause far more problems than it solves.

My girl-friend is putting pressure on me to have sex with her. I feel I may soon give in. By the way, my girl-friend is not a Christian.

We've included this question from the guy's point of view because this kind of question usually comes from girls! Again it shows the great difference in opinion between what 'the world' says about sex, and what God says. As we saw in the survey statistics, very few people in today's society say sleeping together before marriage is wrong. But does that mean the majority is right? Think of what you would say to this guy, and to his girl-friend. How do you avoid the pressure? Would it help to ease off in the relationship, include other people when they go out together? Or should he just break it off? If

A good relationship doesn't depend on sex to keep it going — if it does it isn't real.

you conscientiously pray for the Lord to protect you, will this stop you from giving in? Or does God always allow us freedom to choose, whatever the situation?

Our best advice if you feel you are being pressured by your boy-friend (or vice versa) is to tell them so. Tell them you don't like it. Tell them it goes against what you believe. Tell them it may destroy your relationship if you did give in. And if real love is there, then there will be acceptance. It's not, 'If you love me you would,' but, 'If you love me you wouldn't'. And pray about it, together if you can. For God will strengthen your determination, and give you the strength to choose what you know is right.

6

God and sex

For this reason a man will leave his father and mother and be united to his wife, and they will become one flesh. The man and his wife were both naked, and they felt no shame. Genesis 2:24, 25, NIV.

WAY BACK WHEN . . .

In the past, and maybe even in the minds of some today, the words 'God' and 'sex' should not be part of the same breath. The church has generally been uncomfortable with the physical side of humanity. This attitude has frequently been reflected in its teachings about sex. So while God as Creator must have known what He was doing when He made humankind male and female, and while He also made us capable of experiencing great physical pleasure, all too often church leaders have found it difficult to explain and appreciate God's gift of sexuality.

Of course, just looking for your own pleasure reflects the selfish attitude of sin. That is why the drive for sexual satisfaction can be used to tempt. The Devil knows that better than we do, and he has often used this trap.

It is no accident that ancient religions used sex as part of worship. Sex was a substitute for true religious experience. Cult prostitutes were used to gain an ecstatic feeling; fertility rituals for good crops were linked with sexual acts; in fact sex was made a kind of religion. This is why God had to warn His people against such 'idolatry of sex' throughout the Old Testament. Orgies and 'sacred prostitution' were very much part of the religions of Canaan. God even used these images to illustrate the way His people were so keen to leave Him and follow their own desires. Again and again God speaks of Israel 'playing the harlot'.

One of the most famous examples was in Moab: 'When the Israelites were camped in the Valley of Acacia, the men began to have sexual intercourse with the Moabite women who were there. These women invited them to sacrificial feasts, there the god of Moab was worshipped. The Israelites ate the food and worshipped the god Baal of Peor.' (Numbers 25:1, 2.) The end result of this? A plague that killed 24,000 people. Notice how idol worship and sex go together, and how this is clearly totally opposed to God's ideal for His people.

Many teenagers get their knowledge of sex from their peers in the playground. It's mostly ill-informed and open to abuse.

GOD AGAINST SEX?

Perhaps this is why some have concluded that God was against sex, since there are these warnings in the Old Testament. God spoke against all kinds of sexual perversions, and if that was necessary it seems that some at least were doing these 'detestable things'. However, nowhere does God, through His prophets, imply that the beautiful sexual relationship of man and woman in marriage was anything but good.

Just take a look at the Song of Solomon (all quotes from the Good News Bible):

'Your lips cover me with kisses; your love is better than wine. There is a fragrance about you; the sound of your name recalls it. No woman could help loving you. Take me with you, and we'll run away . . . .' The Woman (1:2-4).

'How beautiful you are, my love; how your eyes shine with love!' The Man (1:15).

'I am weak from passion. His left hand is under my head, and his right hand caresses me.' The Woman (2:5, 6).

'Come then, my love; my darling, come with me.' The Man (2:10).

'My lover is mine, and I am his.' The Woman (2:16).

'How beautiful you are, my love! How your eyes shine with love . . . your hair dances . . . your teeth are white . . . your lips are like a scarlet ribbon . . . your cheeks glow . . . your neck is like the tower of David, round and smooth . . . your breasts are like gazelles . . . how perfect you are!' The Man (4:1-7).

Here, in Scripture, is a celebration of intense, physical human love. Under the inspiration of God, this is part of the Bible. What do we make of it? Are we still embarrassed, or can we see God celebrating the beauty of physical love in the right relationship?

Some of the early church fathers seem to have been offended by the descriptions of human love, and made it an allegory of Christ's love for His church. However, at its heart this book describes, in poetic detail, two human beings expressing God's great gift of intimate love for each other. That this love poem should have been included in the Bible says a great deal about God Himself!

So what went wrong?

Like all of God's gifts to us, sex can be abused and misused. This has happened all too often, perhaps because it *is* so powerful. But this doesn't mean that it should be a taboo subject, whispered about and treated as something dirty. It really is an offence to God to throw such a precious gift back in His face and treat it as something unclean and unwholesome.

We know of too many people whose lives have been devastated by mistaken ideas of the appropriateness of sex. A minister's wife who had been brought up to believe all things sexual were dirty, consequently just endured her husband's attentions. A young lady from a broken home

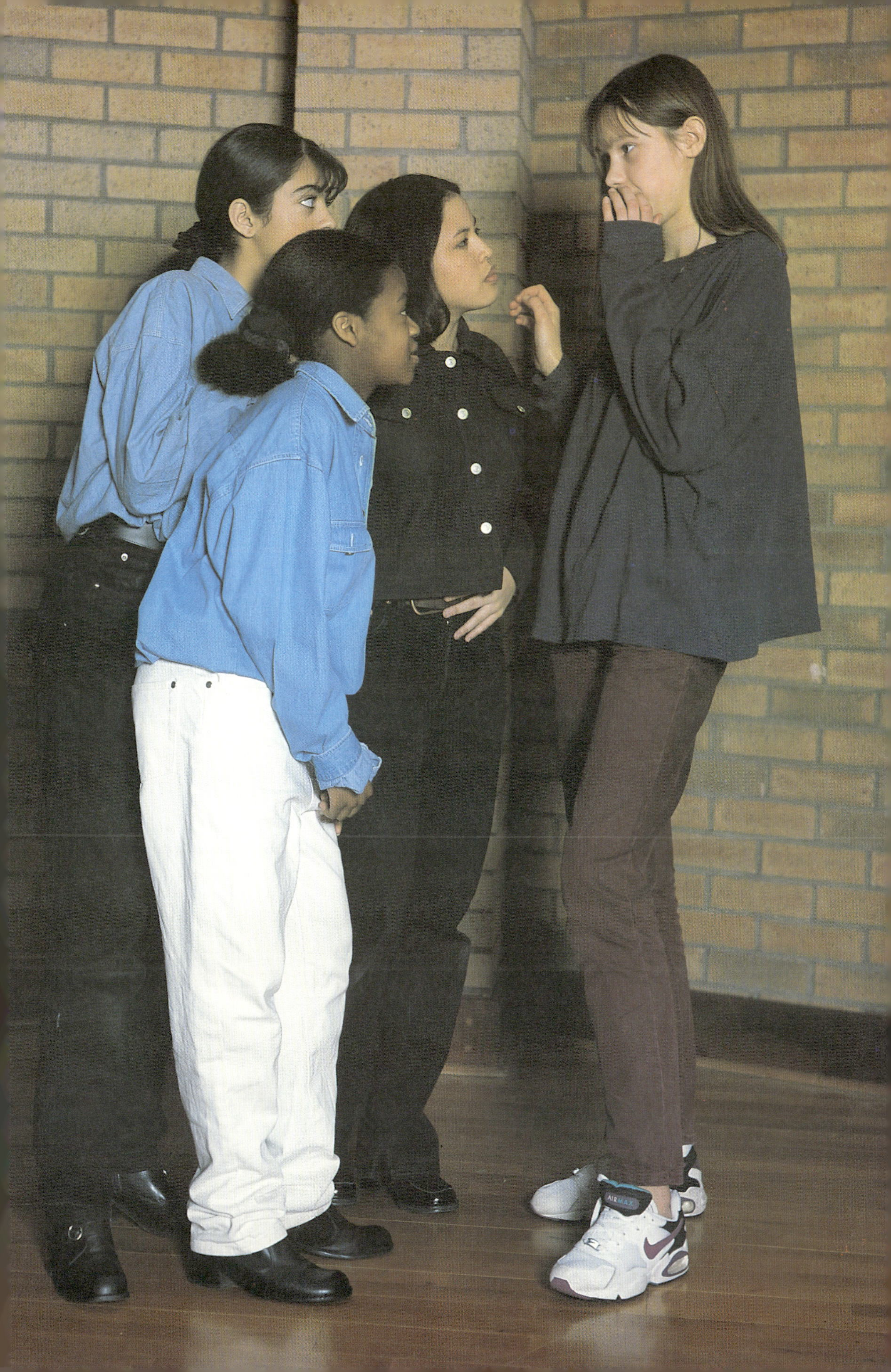
AIR MAX

who equated sexual pleasure with violence. A young man too terrified to date girls because of the filthy things that might happen.

How do such beliefs come about?

ANCIENT TEACHINGS

While such situations are not due to any one cause, the teachings of the church over many years have certainly not helped. See what these famous church fathers believed:

Tertullian wrote about women like this: 'The judgement of God upon your sex endures even today; and with it inevitably endures your position of criminal at the bar of justice. You are the gateway to the devil.'

Chrysostom recorded his opinion: 'Woman: a foe to friendship, an unescapable punishment, a necessary evil.'

Origen was so convinced that sex was evil that he castrated himself.

These men were following beliefs popular in their own society. These beliefs included the idea that there was a pure soul locked inside an evil body. So everything the body did was sinful.

No wonder that so many people have been so confused about sex and how this relates to God. The truth is that God created us as sexual beings. God designed our bodies to experience pleasure, and He wishes that our 'joy may be full'.

But because He wants the very best for us, and not some feeble or false substitute, God has clearly defined the right situation for a sexual relationship. This is not God having a 'down' on sex, or being a kill-joy. Quite the opposite. God cares so much for us and the beautiful gift He has given us that He wants it to be the very best.

SOME STRANGE IDEAS ABOUT SEX!

ARISTOTLE
the philosopher wrote:
'Avoid the inclination to animalistic pleasure, for it stains the soul. Do not yield to the desire for sexual intercourse.'

PYTHAGORAS
taught his students:
'Be sober and chaste. Sex is always harmful and not conducive to health.'

PLATO
perhaps the most famous philosopher of all, believed that:
'Bodily pleasures are slavish, and the true philosopher abstains from them.'

HIPPONAX
noted:
'There are two days when a woman is a pleasure: the day one marries her and the day one buries her.'

JUST FOR HAVING KIDS?

Linked to such negative ideas about physical sex has been the idea that it was only intended to keep the human race going: sex is for procreation only. Once again this idea did not originate in the church, but gradually seeped in.

A couple of examples, this time from Latin writers:

'Sexual desire has been given to man not for the gratification of pleasure but for the continuance of the human race.' *Seneca*.

'We should not have sexual connection for the sake of pleasure, but only for the sake of begetting good children.' *Lucanus*.

Put together these ideas and, pretty soon, sex ends up just as a necessary evil, something that has to be done as a duty in order to have children. And the natural result of this was celibacy — avoiding sex altogether — the concept that to be really holy you gave up any thought of sex. Eventually this idea is what led to the monasteries and convents.

The idea that sex is purely to keep the population going is not a Christian idea. A secure, close, loving relationship, enjoying an active sex life is God's way to produce loved and balanced children.

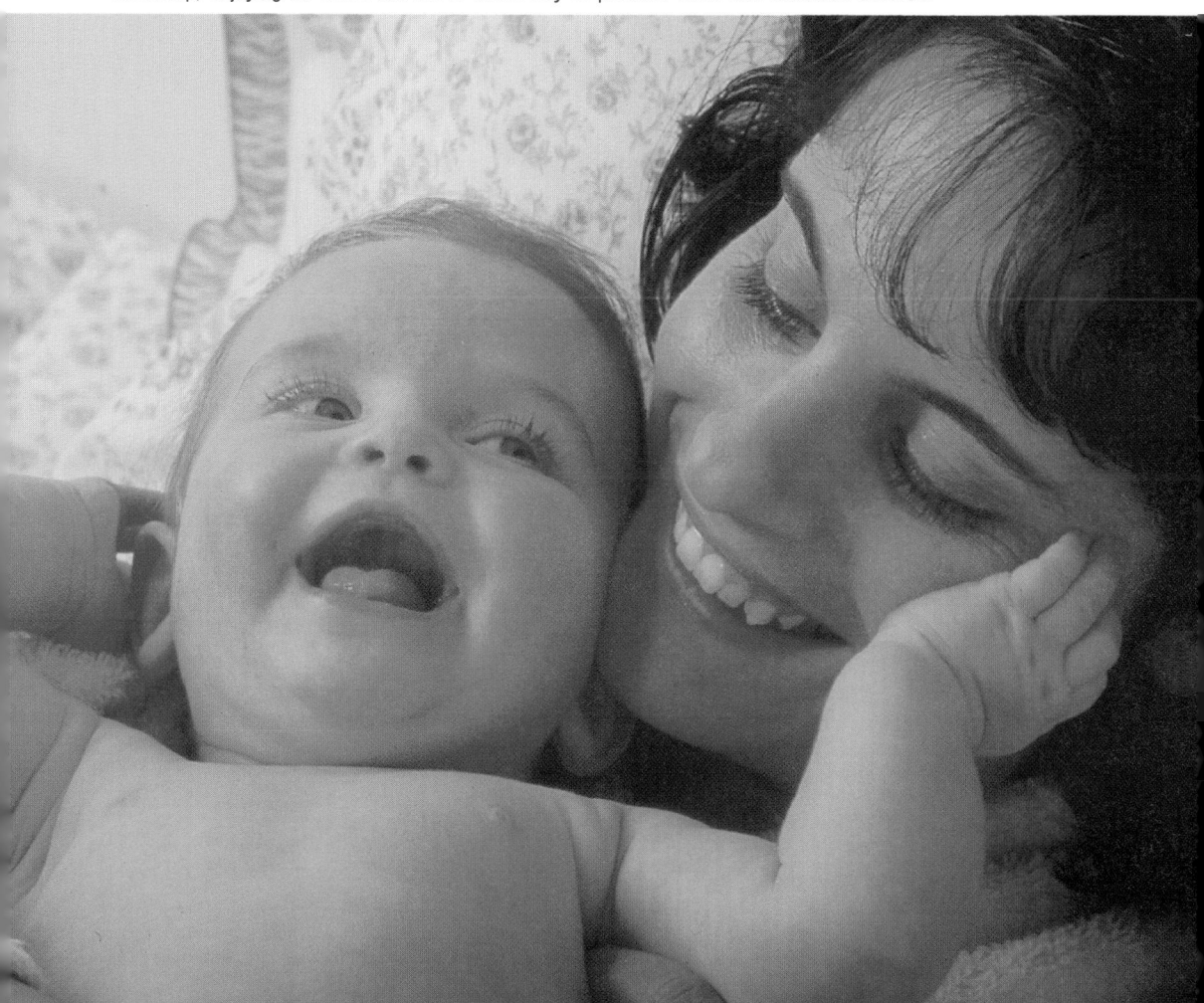

Whatever happened to God's plan for sexual joy in a happy relationship? For centuries it lay rotting in the gutters of side streets, consigned to brothels, rarely spoken of and generally despised. Another tragedy of mistaken ideas of God and His purposes.

THE BEGINNING

What Jesus said about divorce — often a sexual breakdown — also applies to debased ideas of sex: 'In the beginning it was not so.' God did not intend us to relate to each other this way. Broken relationships are a result of sin.

So how was it? Man was made in God's image (see Genesis 1:27). If man is made in God's image, does that include human sexuality? That concept really *does* make you stop and think.

And what about Eve? The Bible records that it was not good for man to be alone. This shows us that only through being together — including the sexual union — could humanity become complete.

The Bible uses a very special word for sex. It shows us the intimacy and understanding that God intends for sex. Look at some of the King James Bible's statements:

Adam knew Eve his wife; and she conceived. Genesis 4:1.
Cain knew his wife; and she conceived. Genesis 4:17.
Adam knew his wife again; and she bare a son. Genesis 4:25.
He knew her again no more. Genesis 38:26.
She knew no man. Judges 11:39.
Elkanah knew Hannah his wife . . . she bare a son. 1 Samuel 1:19, 20.
But the king knew her not. 1 Kings 1:4.
(Joseph) knew her not till she had brought forth her firstborn son. Matthew 1:25.

KNOWING

You can see that the word 'knew' is used in all these places in the Bible to describe sexual intercourse, the most intimate way of knowing. In fact the meaning would be very strange if we understood it any other way. What kind of woman doesn't know any men as it might seem to say in Judges 11:39? And in the story of David and his 'bed-warmer' Abishag, the record states that 'the king knew her not'. Does this mean that the woman in his bed was a stranger and they weren't introduced?

No. This is what was called in the old days 'carnal knowledge'; that gaining of the most private of human knowledge. This 'knowing' reflects the fact that the physical aspects of sex should only be part of a full and intimate relationship, a closeness that is further explained as becoming 'one flesh' (Genesis 2:24; Ephesians 5:31).

'A man who loves his wife loves himself. (People never hate their own bodies. Instead, they feed them and take care of them, just as Christ

The relationship between a man and a woman in self-giving love is a great illustration of how God wants to relate to us.

does the church; for we are members of his body.) As the scripture says, "For this reason a man will leave his father and mother and unite with his wife, and the two will become one." There is a deep secret truth revealed in this scripture, which I understand as applying to Christ and the church.' (Ephesians 5:28-32.)

What an amazing thought! That the link between Christ and us as members of the church is symbolized by the sexual union of man and wife! How could God have a negative view of sex when He even uses this as a symbol of the intimate relationship between Christ and the church?

In the same way that sex physically joins two bodies together so that they become 'one', then two minds, two complete beings become 'one', united, unified in goals and purposes. And interestingly, this is what God says He wants with us — to become 'one' — united, at one with each other (see John 17:21-26).

The relationship of man and woman in self-giving love is used by God as the best description He can find for the relationship He wants with each of us. It is based on total trust, it has no secrets, it is very intimate. The church is the 'bride of Christ' (Revelation 21:9), the object of His supreme love, and the church includes you and me.

It's clear then that God is not a killjoy. He just wants our pleasure to be the best it can — and this can't be part of a guilty, hidden association or a one-night stand.

God's ideal is expressed right there at the beginning: 'For this reason a man will leave his father and mother and be united to his wife, and they will become one flesh. The man and his wife were both naked, and they felt no shame.' (Genesis 2:24, 25, NIV.)

So where did the shame come from at the Fall? Was it linked with sex? When they saw each other naked and they were ashamed, was it because of hidden sexual desires?

No. The Bible makes it clear that the actions of sin result from the breakdown of a relationship. When Eve chose to believe the serpent and not God, her relationship with God was severely damaged. Likewise with Adam in his conscious choice. The shame comes from the breakdown of the relationship and the realization of what this sin is, not from some kind of sexual embarrassment.

And when we truly do *make love* in the right meaning of those words, when we try to recreate that experience that God planned for us back in Eden, then our sexual union is teaching us something of what it really means to be one with God. And being one with God is being brought back into love and trust, the ending of sin through the restoration of the relationship, the reconciliation that only God can give. See why the right ideas about God and sex are important!

God is right there in your relationship, whether you acknowledge Him or not. So why not speak to Him about your hopes and fears, your guilt and your desire? For a true love relationship with a man must involve the God who is Love — true, honest and real love.

QUESTIONS AND ANSWERS

What's wrong in being sexy if God made us that way?

Depends on what you mean by 'sexy'! You can't excuse all kinds of actions just because 'God made me that way'. That's a cop-out. But it is true that God designed the human body to appreciate beauty and love, pleasure and desire. This all has to be contained, however, in the right relationship. As someone once said, 'Sex is not a nice way to say hello.' You can't live in a promiscuous or even a flirtatious life-style and not be affected by it. Actions have consequences. Even sexy thoughts have their inevitable results.

If God really loves us, why doesn't He let us do what we want — you know, sexually?

Is it loving to let your son run out under a bus, and not try to stop him? Is it loving to let your daughter play with rusty razor blades, and not try to take them away from her? And anyway, if you really want to do as you please, God won't stop you. He just wants you to be sure of what the consequences will be.

For God has a better plan than anything you can think of. You may believe that to have sex with your boy-friend is going to be the very best thing ever. But is it? What will be the situation? What if he decides afterwards he prefers someone else? What if he only pleases himself and doesn't bother about you, will that be fun? And most of all, what will sex be to you afterwards? Just some physical thing, or will it be the high-point of a life-time relationship that involves not just the physical, but the mental and spiritual too? We are convinced that God really loves us, and so He wants us to find our greatest joys in what He knows will be the best and most fulfilling way.

My teacher at school says my religion has made me 'repressed'. What does this mean?

Unfortunately this means that your teacher doesn't really understand God and sex. Now it may be that your teacher has had some experiences of religious people who have had sexual hang-ups, and thinks that those hang-ups have resulted from what the church teaches. And it may even be that your upbringing, or what you have learned in church about sex, has made you think it is something bad. But because some of us misunderstand God's intentions for our sexuality doesn't mean God is wrong.

By saying you are 'repressed', your teacher is suggesting that you have some sexual fears that make you inhibited; you don't want to share yourself, you don't want to express how you feel. This may be part of your personality, but it's important to understand that God says His design for your sexuality is good.

> When God says 'no', it's not to be awkward, He's trying to point out that what you look upon as freedom is a trap that prevents you experiencing the best in human experiences.

God wants the best for you, and you should perhaps find someone you respect and trust — who is open and yet responsible — with whom to discuss some of these more intimate matters.

Why did God say 'No' and make it so difficult?

Did He? Of course the physical drive can be very powerful, but it's like asking why do car makers put powerful engines in their vehicles? It's all a question of the use to which the vehicle is put and the direction you take. However, if you are very free in your mutual enjoyment and things are getting 'out of hand', then obviously it will become increasingly difficult to say 'No'. Very often when such questions are asked it is because just about every physical step has been taken short of intercourse, and then to say 'No' just before that point is frustrating and difficult. Also remember that God is not just saying 'No'. What He is saying 'No' to is something that is not going to benefit you or your partner — certainly in the longer term. Remember that the feelings of guilt that result from ignoring God's advice are more to do with the realization that you have 'sold yourself short', that what should have been part of a beautiful scene has been a sordid moment, that it was so 'incomplete'. More than one person in that situation has told us that 'It just wasn't enough; I wanted it to mean much more than that' — and it's true. For the actual physical act is not what really satisfies; it's what it *means* to both of you. And if the meaning is degraded, then so is your relationship and its basis.

Doesn't God's displeasure with Onan in his spilling his seed on the ground indicate that He opposes birth control? Gen. 38:8-10.

Read this story and you find out that God was not angry about birth control but because Onan was deliberately disobeying God's way of providing for his late brother's family. We cannot use texts that are describing one idea and use them for another. There is nothing in this story to say that God is opposed to birth control and, indeed, the emphasis is on the principle of making sure a family can be provided for. So on principle, God seems to be saying the very reverse: that He is more concerned over making sure children that are brought into the world are properly cared for, which would indicate that if we cannot be sure to do that, birth control would be better.

Kissing is an enjoyable activity. Should it only take place between man and wife or boy-friend and girl-friend, or can it take place between anyone you feel attracted to, bearing in mind one's Christianity?

It's good that you say you enjoy kissing. It's important to admit what we feel, and not to deny that we like the feelings. What is appropriate is another question, and it also depends on what type of kiss. The Bible tells us to 'Greet each other with a holy kiss'. So what kind of kiss is that? And you know very well

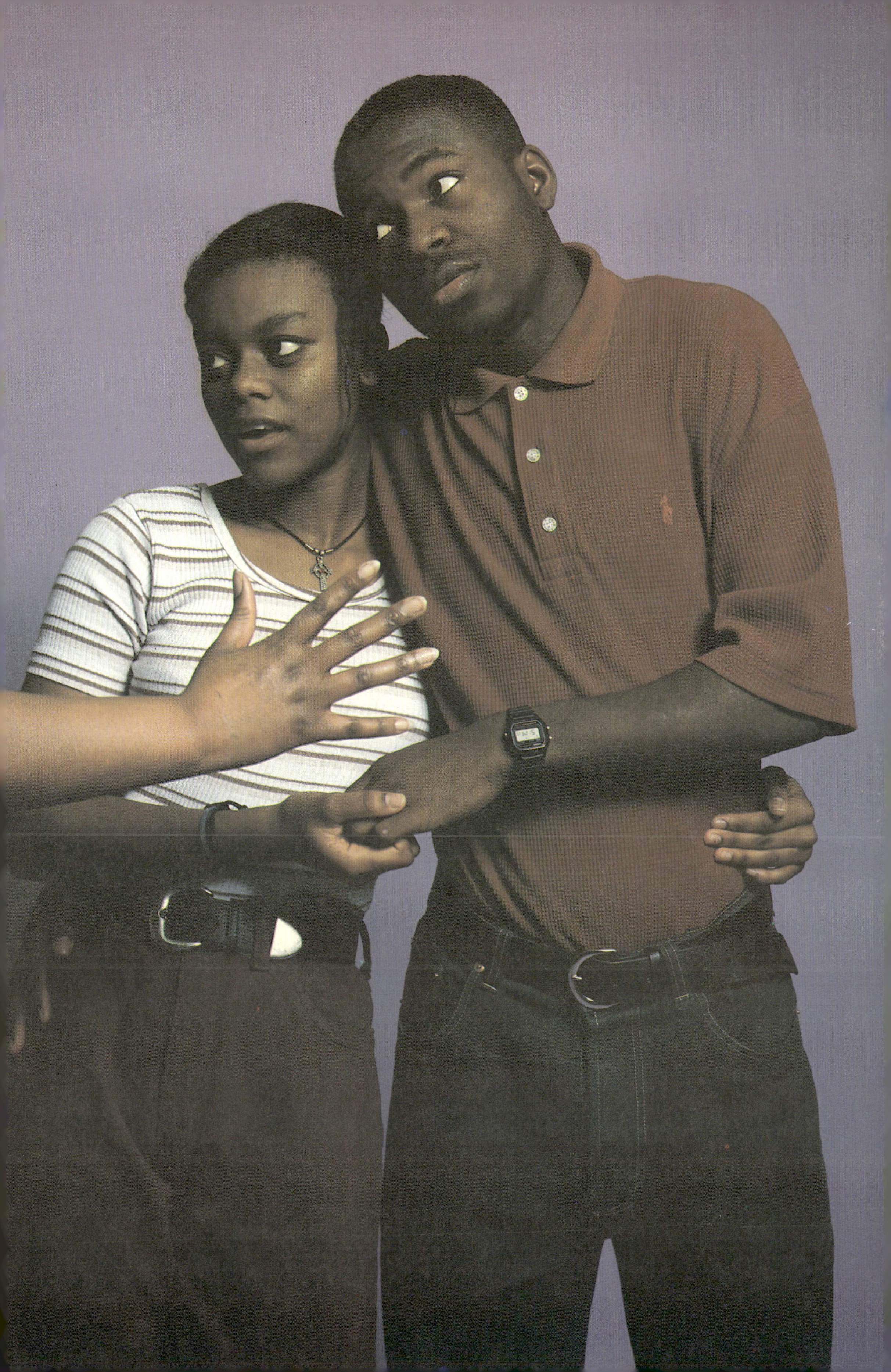

that the kiss you give your boy-friend is not the same kiss you give your father.

Sometimes Christians get the idea that they shouldn't even kiss before they get married. The trouble with that idea is that it doesn't last long. The danger is then to think, 'Well, I've broken my principles here, I might as well give up and do everything.'

Don't make promises you can't keep. We would suggest that kissing your boy-friend is not wrong — but that even here you need to keep a lid on things. For extended sessions can easily lead to more than kissing, and you tend to want to go further every time. As to going around kissing everybody — keep your special kisses special, and if you do kiss others (to greet them, for example) then make sure it's on the cheek!

If, as you say, sex isn't dirty, why do I feel uncomfortable thinking God will be watching?

The need for privacy shouldn't be associated with something being dirty. Of course couples will wish to be alone, for intimate behaviour is just that — it does not and should not include anyone else. Nor is God some kind of Peeping Tom who will be spying on you. In any case, why should you feel uncomfortable if God made you and sees you as you are, and put in you the wonderful ability to enjoy sexuality and to give pleasure too? Of course if you're misusing sex or in some other way acting against what God has said, then you should feel uncomfortable! But if you are acting within God's defined framework, following His advice (which is for your best good), then accept the gracious goodness of God, and don't worry about looking over your shoulder.

How do sexual matters affect the church?

In a wide variety of ways, some

Living with the constant fear that God has your behaviour under scrutiny is only for those who abuse His guidelines.

direct, and some indirect. How the church handles sexual sin and deviation is an obvious question, and calls for great wisdom. Less obvious but equally real is the impact that sexual problems have on the church through defective relationships and broken families. Many difficulties within the church may not be obviously due to sex, but frustrations in this area are often brought over into other areas of life. A number of churches we know have been so affected, and we believe that if this vital area of human experience was improved, so would be church life generally! That's the negative. On the positive side, an appropriate attitude to sexuality will make the church more relevant, more able to help, and more able to rightly portray a gracious God to a sad and dying world.

How are Christians to deal with sex in a sex-mad world?

The Christian reaction must be balanced. To close our minds to what is happening in the world is practically impossible, and simply to shut it all out may mean for some denying sexuality altogether. Nor, very obviously, should we run headfirst into this sex-mad world, as you call it. Christians need to see again the God-focused nature of sex, and praise and thank Him for it. It's not something we dreamed up; sex is not a human invention. It came from God, and it is for our good. The Devil has taken sex and perverted and debased it, but we do not need to follow such ideas. Rather, we need to promote God's gift of sexuality as part of His plan for humanity, as a wonderful expression of true love between a man and a woman, not just some slaking of lust or self-satisfaction.

What about the church's attitude to sins and sexual sins? Are they any different?

It sometimes seems that way, doesn't it? Perhaps sexual sins are more visible; or is it that they seem to threaten people more? Whatever the case, sexual sins have frequently been viewed in the church as particularly bad. However, we must keep a proper perspective here, whatever our own personal reaction to sexual sins. Does God see them as being particularly different from other vices? Sin is sin, some say — and there's truth in that. On the other hand, the impact of sexual sin on relationships can be so severe that they do have a major practical impact, and the church does well to treat such very seriously. Of one thing we're sure — there is no sin that God cannot forgive — except for the sin you don't want forgiven.

Should the church be involved in speaking about sex?

Yes, absolutely. In the past, the church may not have expressed itself very well, but that's no reason to give up. Besides, if the church doesn't speak, there are many others who will, and their ideas about sex may be a long way from what the Bible teaches. While Christians are right to emphasize the intimate nature of sex, to remain silent is very dangerous and foolish, especially when the world's view is so very different.

GOD-NONSENSE

Some Christians have some very odd ideas about God and His relationship to our sexuality. Think how you would try to answer some of these ideas (some suggestions are given to help you):

God doesn't say anything in the Bible about deep kissing or masturbation or oral sex. So what God doesn't forbid must be OK.

Neither does God say anything about computer games or horror videos or drugs or smoking or . . . . But there are plenty of principles you can work from.

God is against sex because it was involved in Adam and Eve's sin with the apple.

God nowhere speaks against sex as an expression of love between husband and wife. The story in Genesis says nothing about sex being involved in the Fall. And it doesn't say it was an apple either!

If you are really sorry about having sex with your boy-friend God will forgive you and prevent you getting pregnant.

Yes, God can and does forgive. In fact, He is usually more loving and forgiving than we are, especially with sexual sin. But He doesn't take away the consequences since that was your choice.

God only made sex for reproduction.

So if you enjoy it, then you're sinning? Why then did God make us beings able to enjoy pleasure, especially making our sexual organs that way?

The church shouldn't be involved in sex education.

What happens when it isn't? If this is true, then the use of one of our most powerful drives may be under the influence of those with no principles at all. And isn't God to have a voice in every part of our lives?

If you have sex with someone, you are married in God's eyes.

Nowhere does the Bible say that. It does say that sexual intercourse forms a union between two people. But that does not mean to say that once you have had sex then you have to get married, or that God will curse you if you don't. You may even make the mistake worse if you do marry.

Christians have a lot less trouble with sex than other people.

We wish that were true, but it isn't. All the studies show that young people in the church have the same kind of problems and questions as those outside the church. Sometimes there are more difficulties; for example a Christian couple do not expect to have intercourse, and when they 'accidently' go too far, they may not have used contraception since they were not prepared. This may explain the higher than average rate of unmarried teenage pregnancies among some Christian groups.

Christians only need to pray about it and God will take away their sexual urges.

God doesn't work by taking away choices. God is a God of freedom and, while He helps us to make the right choices, He doesn't remove our right to choose. Besides, when you marry, don't you want your sexual urges?

Sexual desire is a sin.

No. God gave us sexual desire. It is wrong expression which is a sin.

Christian married couples automatically have better sex.

Not automatically. The potential is there, but it depends on their background, their willingness to learn from each other and to explore their sexualities, and how much God's gift of loving sex is allowed to grow in their relationship.

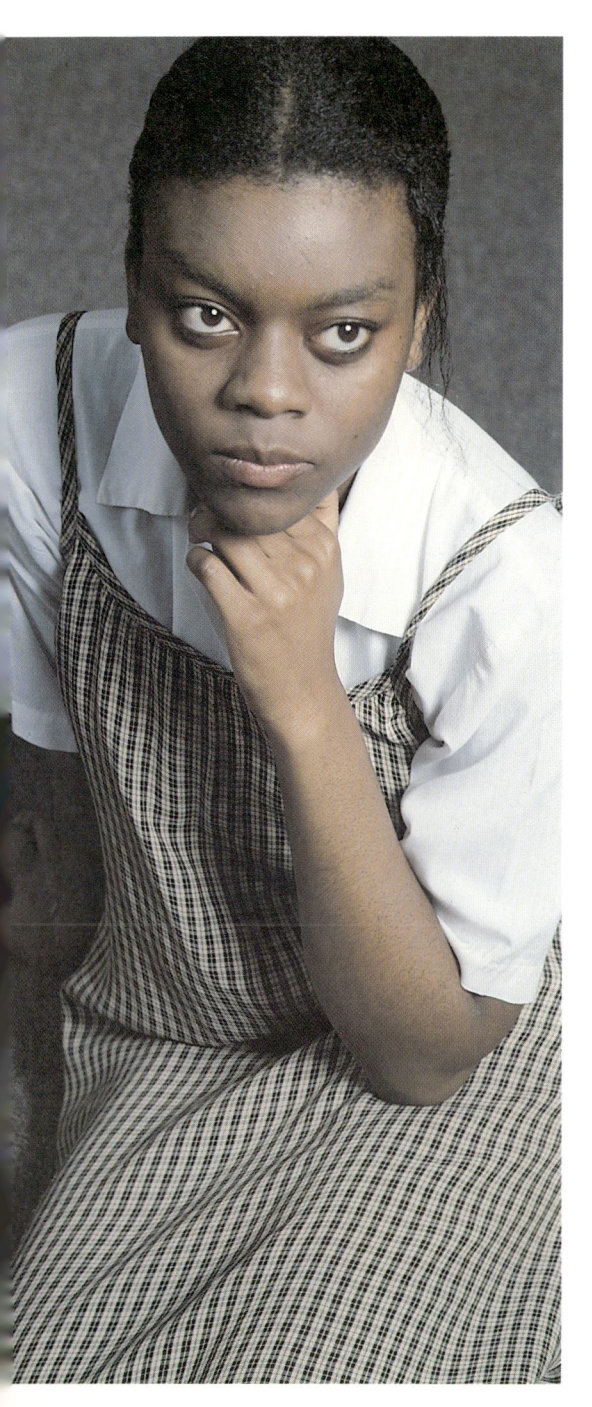

Prayer is not an instant line to instant answers where God overrules your freedom to choose.

7

Putting it into practice

Come then, my love; my darling, come with me. Song of Songs 2:13.

SO WHAT DOES ALL THIS MEAN IN PRACTICE?

Putting *what* into practice, exactly? All that you know about the mechanics of sex? No — the principles we've been talking about, the ideals. Now that we've seen the larger view of sexuality, how does this work out?

One strange fact. Despite all the talk of sex in the media, all the facts and figures that do indicate as a society we're sexually obsessed, and all the hype over affairs and adultery and casual sex, marriage is still alive. More than that, in the same survey that dismally revealed the general acceptance of sex *before* marriage, people still strongly opposed sex *outside* marriage.

In a recent survey in Britain, only 2 per cent thought premarital sex was wrong, but 80 per cent considered extramarital sex to be wrong. In other words, it's OK before, but not after marriage: affairs and adultery are still considered wrong.

So there is still some support for the importance of marriage. Despite all the attacks against God's original plan, many remain committed to marriage as the right arrangement for the intimate relationship of man and woman.

THE MARRIAGE PRINCIPLE

Right from the beginning the model of one man, one wife, has been the intended way of expressing our sexuality.

While there have been many departures from this — polygamy (more than one wife), polyandry (more than one husband), mistresses and concubines, living together — marriage provides the framework to allow the best expression of our desires.

Now because of sin, marriage has been damaged. In addition, not all have the opportunity or desire for marriage. So while it is clear from the biblical record that marriage is God's intention for the fulfilment of male and female sexuality (and to some degree, other human potentialities), we cannot say that marriage is the great ideal for all. For various reasons it just doesn't work out that way, and single people must not feel excluded or discriminated against. Being single is OK too, and has some good scriptural backing, particularly in Paul's advice!

Not to marry and to remain single must not be viewed in the context here as being 'incomplete' or 'unfulfilled'. God made us as individuals, and relates to us in that way. Many singles have the opportunity to show and receive love and affection with family and friends, and live totally happy lives.

Yet it is also true that the expression of physical intimacy — love in sex — unlocks another aspect of human potential and experience. It's not for us to say that one status is better than another, they are simply different, and have different benefits and problems.

So how does all this work? How does this falling in love happen? Do you get to choose, or is the choice already made for you?

BECOMING FRIENDS

Courting, dating, going out, going steady — there are many names for this process of choosing your partner. For the Christian this process is even more significant, choosing for life. The way we go about choosing our mate may seem very bizarre.

Don't feel abandoned if your friends all have boyfriends and you're still looking! To jump into the arms of anyone going free to be in with the crowd can be a bad mistake.

Maybe it even seems that way to you too!

For there is no definite way to date. Ask anyone — and you'll find their experiences are different. That's good, for we all need to discover ourselves and each other in the way that's best for us. The only down side is that there seems to be no way of finding out whether what you're doing is right!

Some suggestions. Don't start with the idea 'I need a man'! Don't even decide that you must have a boy-friend because all your girl-friends have one. Many, many mistakes have been made thinking like that. From our experience, the best relationships are natural ones. By that we mean that they came about by an almost casual process of getting acquainted, and not through a decision to find a husband. Computer dating tries to do this methodically — but no more successfully perhaps — and works by linking people who appear suitable.

And yet even that is simply trying to match 'possibles'. That's what you're doing by getting to know boys — at least on the subconscious level. Sometimes like attracts like, other times difference is exciting. So even in this there are no guarantees. Neither should you go out with a shopping list of your perfect man. (Unless you are the perfect woman, of course!)

But you should have a few ground rules, a few principles. In order to be able to 'become one' both of you

Make friends by beng friendly yourself. Be part of a group who do things together. This way you can find out what 'he' is like without getting involved too deeply.

will need at least some common ground to begin with. And for a Christian, if God is not there, rarely will the relationship be all it should be. Thinking of all the marriages we know of between a Christian and a non-Christian, we can think of only a few that have worked, and even fewer that have worked really well. Sometimes, though rarely, one will convert the other, and a beautiful God-filled relationship can be built. Usually the relationship goes the other way, and often is wrecked on the rocks of our sinful natures.

So think about that. It's not wrong to date a non-Christian, but you have even more to think about if you're going to get serious.

Then there's the common ground of shared interests. Not everything, of course. But at least some similar views on some of the more important subjects (minor things like the meaning of existence, the principles of morality, life objectives — small stuff like that!). Not much chance exists for a good relationship if you're arguing all the time.

We *would* suggest that you place a high priority on certain characteristics like honesty, trustworthiness, sensitivity, sense of humour, consideration, caring, good listening skills, self-assurance, balance — and you can add to the list. *You* know what we're getting at!

HOW TO START?

Think of how you make friends with someone. You say 'Hello', and then make some neutral comments just to see what kind of response you get. If you have seen someone you would like to become more friendly with, then observe. What does he like to do? How does he act? What are his interests? Get someone talking on their favourite subject and you may well still be there next Christmas!

And be prepared for rejections; some more polite than others. Remember that rejection is a universal experience; you're not odd if someone says 'No' to you. If you have to say 'No', then please try not to hurt. Be firm but fair.

> Be prepared for the pain of being rejected. It might seem your world has collapsed but you're not odd — it's a common experience!

Do you know the best way to make friends? By being friendly yourself — and not being nervous and worried about it all. Being convinced that God made you special and that He loves you can do wonders for your self-worth!

So how do you make this general friendship more specific? It's no longer necessarily (thankfully!) the guy who has to make the first approach. Especially if you are part of a group who go out together regularly, you probably have a fair idea of what interests him. Make sure this is not an invitation to anything more than what it should be. You *do* need to avoid giving any wrong impressions. One boy's girl-friend once told him she was on the Pill. He wondered why she told him that. It turned out later she had trouble with heavy periods, and she was letting him know of her difficulty (she thought). Obviously he got the wrong impression.

SITUATIONS!

Don't put yourself in the situation of sitting alone together for long spells in the back of a darkened car, the front-room couch, or in his or your room. It's not going to help either of you or your progressing relationship. Best are the experiences that build friendship — whether it's playing games, or going walking, or working together. When you can go home after a great day together, knowing it was healthy and wholesome, and with nothing to be ashamed about — that's a really good date.

To be together in a beautiful setting when love is in your heart — that surely brings a truer fulfilment than sexual activity which you know is wrong.

'Come then, my love; my darling, come with me. The winter is over; the rains have stopped; in the countryside the flowers are in bloom. This is the time for singing; the song of doves is heard in the fields. Figs are beginning to ripen; the air is fragrant with blossoming vines. Come then, my love; my darling, come with me.' (Song of Songs 2:10-13.)

Would you say no to this invitation? What a delightful thought: to discover together the joy of life, to hear the sound of music in your beloved's voice, to join your whole being with his in the delight of God's love. Reading to one another the Song that Solomon wrote is truly moving, the more so when you realize that this is God's plan for each of us!

INVOLVE GOD

Right from the start, involve God. Talk to Him about your plans — whichever guy you're thinking about. As the relationship develops, try not to be embarrassed about praying with your boy-friend.

Maybe this might be 'Mr Right' and you consider marriage, then you need God even more. You need to be sure in your decisions.

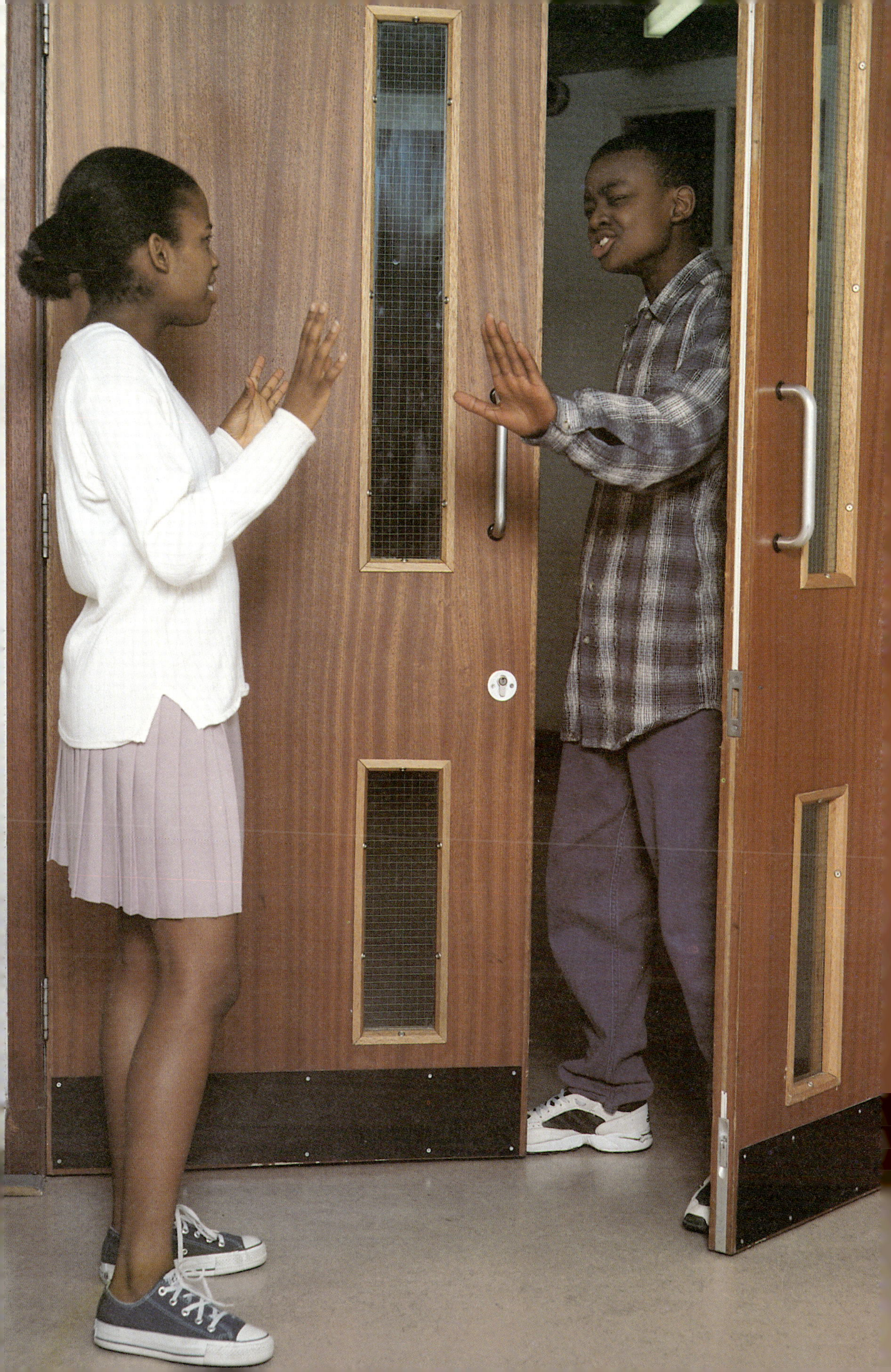

Especially in today's world of sexual indulgence, God can be with you when your emotions are getting out of control. Your body is supposed to be under your control, but sometimes it feels as if it's the other way round. If God is part of your relationship together, then choosing the right may not always be easy, but far more likely!

SO HOW FAR IS TOO FAR?

If you don't know you'll be there before you know it. So it's important to draw the line and decide in advance. Of course it's easy to say that, far harder to do.

How do you tell your boy-friend? Do you get a pen out and start marking lines on your respective bodies? To say, 'You can touch me here but not there', sounds quite odd, doesn't it?

Because of this communication problem, it's easy to leave unsaid things that need to be said. But this can be disastrous. Somehow you need to explain to your boy-friend that you *know* that some actions are going to hurt you both. If he really does love and respect you, he'll go along with you. Don't make him out to be the problem, necessarily. If you're telling him no, and yet all your body actions and behaviour are suggesting you mean yes, you can easily confuse the situation. (That's not a male excuse: just make sure your actions match your words!)

Remember, too, that though sexual activity is an expression of self-

Involve God, right from the start. Learn to pray together over the decisions you are making. Talk to Him about the issues that worry you — and those that don't!

giving love, it can also be extremely selfish. The person (boy *or* girl) who says, 'If you loved me, you would give me what I want' is not operating from Christian principles. That is pure selfishness, wanting your own pleasure at the expense of someone else, and their principles. In the words of Len Barnett, 'Love never storms the gate.'

As we've noted before, making love begins with the first touch — even the first look. We're made to enjoy all these physical acts, and so it's not hard to continue and progress. But where do you stop?

Just to have the line drawn — and by someone else — doesn't help you much. One useful idea is that anything you begin to feel uncomfortable and troubled about is going too far. This shows that your conscience is busy and helping you to stop behaviour that is hurting you. For that's what it's all about — hurting your partner and yourself. It may *feel* good, but that doesn't make it truly good. (You may love the feeling and taste of sweets, but that doesn't mean they're really good! — at least not for your teeth and your body.)

But your conscience may not always be the best guide either. Either through habit or by repressing uncomfortable thoughts you may even fool your conscience into saying, 'There's nothing wrong with that.' So some practical advice.

Don't think that God is saying, 'Don't have sexual intercourse', and that everything else is fine. It's *not* all right to have stimulation almost to climax and then avoid penetration. It's like powering up a space rocket and then trying to shut down the engines just before the announcer says, 'Zero. Blast off!' Nor is it OK to masturbate mutually, or have oral sex — because that's 'Not really intercourse, is it?' Maybe not, but it's a simulation of the real thing and has similar physical effects. And once started as a regular practice, it's very hard to stop. It may even lead to problems later in marriage, in particular if the practice has been over a long period. The mind may get into the habit of thinking that 'this is sex' and can end up preferring it, even in marriage.

Remember what Jesus said about committing adultery in your heart. Sex is more to do with your mind than anything else. For you can't be happy and cheerful when you're doing things you know God forbids. So while love can be expressed in touches and caresses and kisses — and be perfectly good — be careful not to allow yourself to be so wrapped up in your enjoyment that you stimulate each others sexual organs. The physical drive needs careful control (remember to stay in the right gear!), and you want to keep the ultimate form of self-abandonment to God's safe situation of a totally committed and holy union.

For though you may not agree, you only choose to lose control. Many women have said that they, 'Just lost control', as if they couldn't have acted otherwise. But by your decisions up to that point — to do what you did, to allow what you allowed, to stay when you should have left — you decided to become sexually involved.

Don't put yourself or your boyfriend in a situation where it's hard to make the right choice. One girl told of getting so involved with her boy-friend that they had ended up naked on a bed together, and he was about to penetrate her when she suddenly asked him what he was doing. Why hadn't she asked before? Why wait until then? Thank God they both did stop — but she admitted it was *extremely* difficult.

So stop before you start! Realize from what we've said here that it's very difficult to go back, and don't rush to intimacy. If it's right, it will come and make sure it is in the right, true and honest way — the way God intended.

WHEN LOVE GOES WRONG

'I wish I'd know all this before. But now it's too late.' The comment of a girl at a recent seminar we con-

HOW FAR SHOULD I GO?

Notice the question is not how far *can* I go? Being sexually responsible is not about driving at 100 miles an hour towards the edge of a cliff, and then slamming the brakes on to stop going over! Going to the limit every time can be very dangerous too. So you decide where you want to go, and what you *should* do.

Tick whether or not you agree with the statement:

	AGREE	DISAGREE
■ What I do sexually affects me deeply so I need to take this seriously.	☐	☐
■ If I don't know where my behaviour is going, I can get into bad situations.	☐	☐
■ I don't care what happens in sex. If it feels good, I just do it.	☐	☐
■ If you're in love, it doesn't matter how far you go.	☐	☐
■ I think that all you should do with your boy-friend is hold hands.	☐	☐
■ You both need to decide beforehand what is acceptable.	☐	☐
■ Once you start touching each other's genitals it becomes much harder to say no.	☐	☐
■ Touching and kissing each other is important, but you shouldn't spend too long just doing this.	☐	☐
■ If you're both strong, you can withstand any temptation.	☐	☐
■ If you do go too far, there's no point in going back. Just keep on doing what you're doing.	☐	☐

ducted illustrates what we all know: how often things go wrong. For even when we *do* know, how easy it is to put our minds on hold while we enjoy the feelings.

We'll look in more depth at 'God's way back' in a later chapter. For the moment you need to realize that though you know the theory, nobody can ever equip you for that thousand-volt-charge the first time you kiss, and how easily even the most determined Christian can be derailed.

The pressures of dating can lead to bad choices — in guys and in situations. Add in some other factors — like heavy music, discos, alcohol, drugs even — and you have a recipe, not only for disaster, but life-destruction.

Whatever the reasons, you've done it. So because you've done it, you might as well do it again, right? Funny how the devil smilingly springs this 'pleasant' trap on us. First of all, he's busy whispering in your ear, 'Go ahead. Won't hurt you. Why not enjoy it? Go on, it's no big thing. Have some fun.'

And as soon as you do, wham! 'Got you now, my girl. Can't call yourself sweet and innocent anymore, can you? Well, now that you've done this terrible thing, you've had it. There's no way back — might as well be hung for a sheep as a lamb. You might as well keep going.'

No, no, and no! God *still* loves you, *still* wants the best for you, is

The pressures to conform to media hype can lead to poor choices in men and entertainment which can easily wreck your future life.

still right there beside you to help and heal. God doesn't give up on you when you sin sexually any more than He does with any other kind of sin. He may have tears in His voice, but He still pleads with you to come back, to accept His healing forgiveness — the only One who can really help you.

So if you're in that situation, don't give up on God. You need Him now more than ever — to take your brokenness and heal the damage of sin so that He can make you into someone beautiful again.

REASONS FOR WAITING

Here's a list of ten reasons to avoid sex before marriage. Put a number (from 1 to 10) beside each one to indicate how important it is to you. The most important reason is number 1 and the least important reason is number 10.

- [ ] I would feel so guilty.
- [ ] I'm afraid of getting pregnant.
- [ ] I might get some disease or infection.
- [ ] I worry that others might find out.
- [ ] I know God says it's wrong.
- [ ] I want to be a virgin when I get married.
- [ ] I think it will hurt us both emotionally and spiritually.
- [ ] I love him too much not to give him the best — in marriage.
- [ ] I'm afraid as soon as I say yes he'll leave me.
- [ ] I would lose my self-respect.

A SPIRITUAL ROMANCE

You're under many pressures — from your friends, workmates, family, society, boy-friends. Pressure to date, pressure to become involved sexually, pressure to marry.

Why marry anyway? Some girls fall in love with their image of being married and don't even seem to care who they wed! But marriage is not the hearts and flowers of greeting cards, nor the chocolates and bouquets of romantic novels, not even the flickering images of the Hollywood stars. In real life marriage is real work!

You need to look at the whole question of marriage. What are the plus points? And the minus ones? Those who marry just so they can indulge their sexual appetites will find they have much more to contend with! How will you fit in with your husband's plans? How will he fit in with yours? Careers? Babies?

Remember that your love relationship is more than two. God must be there, it must be a 'spiritual romance.' When we've used that expression, some people have reacted rather negatively. 'I don't think God should be involved in all that, do you?' or, 'When I feel like being romantic, I don't want God looking over my shoulder!'

That reaction is understandable. To some degree it depends on the kind of person you think God is. If you see Him like your father or mother, then maybe you wouldn't want Him in the room when you're kissing your boy-friend. Most people in love want to be alone, and that's understandable.

What we're speaking of is the centrality of God to your relationship. Don't leave Him out of your decisions, don't shut Him out of your life — for God wants to be involved in the really *important* areas. For the person you marry will surely change your life, and it may not be for the better.

When it comes to putting it into practice, you need to consult your Maker and Re-maker. God is the designer of you as you are, and He wants you to have the best He has to offer. In looking for a 'spiritual romance' (which is not sitting around at night having religious quizzes!), ask God for His advice, see what He has to say, read the Bible and pray. Don't put yourself into temptation, and look forward to all the glorious things God has prepared for them that love Him, both now and forever.

The glow of romance as you read the tender words of love and affection. It's a pity but marriage can't survive on sentimental words and kisses, it's a relationship built on trust and love — with God's help.

QUESTIONS AND ANSWERS

If you have dreams that you are making love to someone aren't you sinning by doing so? And if so it wouldn't be that bad to do the real thing, would it? If you have these dreams too often are you normal?

How devious is the human mind! If you've thought it, you may as well do it? Certainly Jesus said that you could commit sexual sins in your mind, but He didn't say that if you did that 'it wouldn't be that bad to do the real thing'. So don't be fooled — just because you've thought of something wrong it *does* matter if you then actually carry out that sin.

Dreaming is something else. None of us has much control over our dreams. If you are filling your mind with sexual images through magazines or movies, then maybe you shouldn't be surprised if those same images enter your dreams. If that's what you're doing, stop feeding your mind in this way.

But if your dreams seem to have no real basis in your waking hours, you shouldn't become too preoccupied about them. After all, dreams are dreams, and not reality. Dreams may disturb us since they don't seem to reflect normality. Dream research seems to suggest that the brain is processing information and ideas — some of which we may not even be consciously aware. You should only be concerned about your dreams if they badly affect you, are very repetitious, or continue over a long time. If these apply, then you may want to seek some kind of counselling.

I've tried so often to find a real boyfriend but I can't. What should I do?

We're tempted to say, 'Stop looking.' Sometimes people just try too hard, and then become over-anxious over their apparent lack of success. We remember one girl who asked a similar question. At 16 you think life is passing you by if you can't find a boy-friend. And it's hard to wait. But after a few false starts, she married at 21 and is still happy years later. You can't hurry love, says a song, and for once it's true. Just concentrate on fulfilling your own potential — your own personality, your career, your relationship with God — and don't rush your love life.

Are sexual thoughts wrong? How can we judge?

How do you define your sexual thoughts? Are they, 'He looks really handsome', or, 'I want to imagine sex with that guy'? Applying what Jesus said about looking that became mental adultery should help. Any thought that demeans the other person, that takes away their humanity and makes them an object — that we would see as being mistaken.

But if you are simply daydreaming — and maybe you are particularly excited by your body's hormone

Don't become over-anxious if you don't have much success in attracting a male. Some people just try too hard!

factory — then don't become plagued with guilt for having immoral thoughts. In the same way as we differentiate between artistic depictions of the human body and pornography, you can judge by your motives and the consequences. Ask God to make sure your sexual thoughts are kept pure, and don't let your fantasies get out of control.

What does it mean 'Better to marry than to burn'?

Paul is speaking about burning with passion, and if such physical desire is getting out of hand, it is best handled in the context of marriage. Of course he's not saying that marriage, purely because of burning, is such a good idea — it's just the better course, since if you feel that way you may end up doing something disastrous. If you marry just for sex, it may be difficult to sustain your marriage for your lifetime.

Why is it important to be a virgin before you get married?

Sometimes the subject of virginity is approached with the idea of the male wanting to possess the best, not wanting 'damaged goods' and so on. Such ideas go back to times when women were virtually sold into marriage and became the man's possession. Such arguments are hardly Christian, and should not be part of any reasoning today.

Yet virginity — for both man and woman — is still God's ideal. Your first sexual experience is designed to be memorable, both physically and mentally. You need love and tenderness, you need more than plain sexual passion. Your gift of virginity is linked with the giving of yourself in the ultimate way. You are special, and you don't want your most complete sexual experience to be anything but special either. Your first time will be the beginning of a long, and we hope happy, sexual journey with your husband. No guilt. No second thoughts. No doubts. No regrets. No past to be anxious over, just a future life together.

Is age important when considering marriage?

Yes, it's one aspect you need to consider seriously. Firstly age generally — there are obvious problems that relate to immaturity and undeveloped personalities. You need to be sure of who you are, and of your partner. The idea of 'growing apart' is often used as an excuse, but it's still a real factor, especially if one or both of you are very young. That's not to say that marrying young will not be successful; just that you need to make sure that your love and commitment are genuine and mature. (On the other hand, there's also the problem of becoming too set in your ways if you leave marriage until much later in life.) But perhaps your question is over a *difference* in age — when one partner (usually but not always the male) is much older. You need to ask yourself other kinds of questions if you're thinking about marrying a man considerably older than yourself. Is he really a substitute father-figure? for example. Or are you just looking for a maturity you don't find in boys your own age? Are you sure he's not exploiting your youth and inexperience? What is his past history? What about possible children — and their perception of an old father? What will happen down the line, since he will arrive at old age much sooner than you? Age — like questions of nationality, race, background, language and so on — is not an insurmountable barrier, but you do need to be aware of these possible complications to your relationship and the reactions of others.

Some people have a long courtship relationship. Can this lead to sex outside of marriage?

As always, it depends. Depends on you and him. For some, the question doesn't arise, since even a short courtship ends up in sex before marriage. But because of our sexual makeup, there are practical difficulties in extending the courtship process. As we've seen, the human sexual response develops over the duration of a relationship. The drive is to go further every time you meet. So by putting off a decision for marriage, or making the date way off in the future, you will experience temptations that for some become increasingly difficult to withstand. This also depends on your previous experience, your sex drive and the attitude your partner takes. But even with the best will in the world from both sides, a long-extended physical relationship (kissing, cuddling, petting) without sex is hard to maintain, and so make sure you make the right decisions about when you marry. Better experience the problems of marriage even when they're inconvenient for your career or whatever, than end up with the guilt and shame of pre-marital sex.

What is the ideal courtship and marriage?

There isn't one! What works for one couple may be boring or stupid or weird for another. The combination of events, reactions and experiences that make up a courtship are special because of the person you're with.

Of course, some may want to define the ideal: boy meets girl, they fall in love, they marry, they live happily ever after. But we're in a real world, with real problems. The ideal is to be the best person you can be, with God's help. The ideal is not to compromise your principles. The ideal is to find someone who shares your beliefs about the real fundamental aspects of life. The ideal courtship and marriage has God at its centre.

Is it wrong for a person to sleep in the same bed with someone else of the opposite sex, bearing in mind no sexual activity has taken place, is taking place, or will take place in the future?

Don't be so foolish. Unless there are extremely compelling reasons you have not explained, this situation is ridiculous. It's not wrong, you are simply putting temptation before you both. How do you know 'no sexual activity . . . will take place in the future'?

Go back to your own bed — alone!

How far is too far? I mean kissing, touching. How far should one go when one wishes to show affection by caressing?

These questions are just two examples of what is probably the most frequently asked question at relationship seminars. Everybody wants specific definitions: you can kiss, but don't use your tongue. You may touch, but only on the hands and face. Kisses should not be longer than 30 seconds. You should never be alone together for more than 5 minutes.

Maybe such rules help some couples. The trouble with some rules is that once you've broken one, and your self-esteem is shattered, you tend to give up and allow it all to happen. What you really need is some true maturity and mutual understanding. Say to yourself, I'm not going to excite him deliberately. I am going to make sure I don't get into any situation in which we may both lose control. Trying to restrain yourself by lying naked on a bed together is like opening a box of chocolates and telling a 2-year-old not to eat any! Why do it?

Be aware of the areas that are especially sensitive for sexual stimulation: the breasts, genitals, thighs and buttocks. Be aware too of the visual signals you are giving out — especially in warm weather when clothing is less. You go to meet your boy-friend in micro cutoffs and a T-shirt with no bra. Clever, or not?

God hasn't given us a rule book in this area. Why not, if it's so important? We believe it's because He wants to treat us as we would want — as adults. So let's act like adults, and operate from Christian principles of self-control, considering the other's needs and fragility, and 'whatsoever things are good, pure, etc' think on these things.

And if you do go too far, go back.

Why is marriage such hard work?

Looking in from the outside it does seem that way, doesn't it? Like any meaningful relationship however, it's worth it. For at the heart of marriage is loving, caring friendship — which should be valued more than anything. That's why you should make sure you choose wisely, talk to God about it, and once decided, determine that this is *for ever!* When two different beings come together to become one, there will be problems to overcome and situations to resolve. But one thing we can assure you — it's worth it!

8

Problems – and solutions

Love must be completely sincere. Hate what is evil, hold on to what is good. Romans 12:9.

THE FUNDAMENTALS

So what's the solution to the problems of sex? For if there's any aspect of Christian life that seems a long way from the theory, it's sex. Through conducting many seminars in youth groups and churches, we have realized that for most young people this is the area of greatest struggle. So if you have a problem you're struggling with, you're certainly not alone.

That's not to condone or to excuse sin. We need to remember the fundamentals we've looked at.

▶ God has defined marriage as the appropriate sanctuary for sexual expression.

▶ We hurt ourselves and others by allowing our selfish urges to take control.

▶ We need to resist the subtle temptations this sex-obsessed world throws at us.

If you know you're not right, you will not help yourself by ignoring the problem, or to saying it's OK when it's not. Sin must still be called by the right name, and not excused by some modern psychological apology — calling it 'maladjustment' or 'inherited guilt' or 'misguided morality'.

For any expression of sexuality that takes you into intercourse (including the substitutes) the Bible describes as *fornication*, and speaks against very clearly. Remember again that this is *not* because God is anti-sex but because inappropriate sexual activity does not fulfil your potential as a complete human being and a friend of God.

THE PAIN OF FAILURE

In one survey of Christian attitudes conducted by a Christian magazine, one in six of the readers that responded had experienced sex outside of marriage, and a massive 91 per cent felt regret or guilt.

While non-Christian counsellors may identify this guilt as brought on by moral principles they think are beside the point, to say 'get rid of God and you'll get rid of guilt' is not an answer. Pain, guilt, sorrow, suffering, bitterness — all these emotional consequences reflect not just a breaking of the rules, but a sense of failure, compromise, and a lessening of self-worth.

One of the saddest, most painful questions was one we received anonymously during a relationship seminar. Written in shaky writing on a piece of paper torn out of a notebook, it simply said:

'If you have gone too far, that is, full sexual intercourse, how do you get rid of the immense pain and guilt feelings, even though you know God has forgiven you? Practical advice please!'

How do you get rid of such feelings? Do they ever go away? Is there healing of the pain? In a later chapter we'll look in more detail at sexual healing. But for the moment make a note of the great pain that can come from wrong sex.

Part of the problem is that you may be unsure what is really wrong with sex outside of marriage — especially if you're planning to marry anyway. For if you're not sure, what will stop you?

You can experiment with some of the negative aspects in life. You know what happens because you have tried it. Because you've burned yourself a few times, you don't need to put your arm into a fire to find out what it does. Because you've fallen over enough you know it isn't a good idea to jump off a cliff. You have felt pain, and it helps!

But what about sex? Especially when there's people around telling you, 'Hey, try it! You don't know what you're missing!' (True enough, you don't know what you're missing — and maybe what you're missing isn't good anyway!)

The Devil used that kind of technique on Eve: 'You don't know what will happen to you if you eat the fruit. I'm telling you God is just stopping you from having something good. I know, I'm tasting the fruit, and it's great!'

Many young people have told us

Do you have to take drugs to find out what the effects will be?

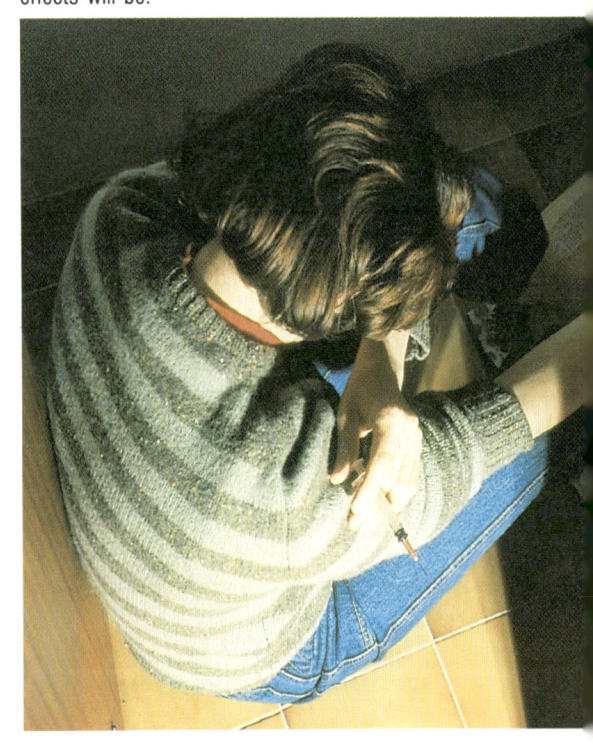

So many teens charge into sexual adventures without a thought, only to find the excitement short lived and hurt long lived.

that their first experience of sexual intercourse was a great disappointment. We're not surprised. Because of all the hype, you think it's going to be like going to heaven. What you're *not* told is that sex is supposed to be part of a total trusting and confident relationship — and that without the whole package the biological coupling is hardly satisfying.

But the question remains — how will I know unless I try it? Well, think about it. Do you have to take drugs to see their effects? Do we have to do everything ourselves, and not learn from the experience of others? And be careful not to believe all you're told — for few people are honest to admit that their sexual relationships are a disaster!

WHAT'S WRONG WITH SEX BEFORE MARRIAGE?

So what is really *wrong* with premarital sex? A few specific answers:
▶ You enter a mutual process of physical dependence. In other words you get hooked on sex. Once you start it's hard to stop. This process can be self-destructive. You feel that you have to give into your body's cravings. You unleash a very powerful force in a situation that is far

from safe. It's easy to get out of control.

▶ You take away from yourself and your partner the whole experience of married commitment. For sex is more than a genital connection; it is meant to express the specialness you have for each other. Through sex you are truly giving of yourself, saying 'I am here to stay. I am not interested in a brief encounter. I want a permanent, enduring and totally trusting relationship.' And when you think of what *can* happen through sex, this is the only way it should be.

▶ You sell yourself short. You are saying to yourself: 'I'm not so important, not so special.' You may even believe that he will leave unless you give him what he wants. (And the one who threatens to go unless he gets it will probably go once he has got it!) What a tragic reason, one that leaves you sickened with yourself. As one preacher once said, 'You can't think crooked and live straight.' You must believe yourself special to God, and not be willing to choose anything but the best. Premarital sex cheapens any relationship, never enhances it.

▶ You can sow seeds of doubt and distrust. We know of marriages that have failed due to insecurity over what the other partner might do, since they had sex before marriage. One husband confessed: 'She did it with someone else before me. Can I be sure she won't do it again?'

▶ Most importantly of all, you are giving away what you cannot give. In Ephesians Paul uses intercourse as a symbol of union — the union we can have with God in the same way as the Father and Son are one. Without
— the totality of trust
— deep commitment
— the wonderful intensity of two beings fusing together
— without all that sexual union is supposed to be, how can you talk about becoming 'one flesh'?

Like secretly opening Christmas presents early, like cheating in an exam, like stealing money from the church collection plate — we end up hurting ourselves. In one Christian survey, over half who admitted to premarital sex said it affected subsequent marriage for the worse. Doubt. Guilt. Distrust. Betrayal. Shame. Uncertainty. Suspicion. All possible results of experiencing sex at second- (or even third-) best.

All of which applies even if you're engaged and plan to marry shortly. For many engagements are broken (more than half, according to one survey), and if you were so confident that you engaged in sexual intercourse — then what? No wonder such experiences can be so shattering, and leave you feeling as if you've been divorced.

The argument 'Tomorrow we'll be married, so it doesn't matter now' reveals a trivial way of looking at a relationship. If someone is so special that you're marrying him, what is one more day to wait? The argument is stronger the other way!

Many engagements don't survive and it can feel like a divorce if you have compromised sexual principles.

BETTER OR WORSE?

As a relationship continues, and especially over a long time, the drive towards intimacy can seem almost overwhelming. It's then that some couples fall into alternative sexual practices. They may say these are better than full intercourse. Because of a decision that intercourse would be wrong, they argue that as long as the penis does not penetrate the vagina, it's OK.

Repeated stimulation that is not satisfied can itself cause intense problems. Stress and tension upset the relationship until some way of resolution is found, either by actual intercourse, or through mutual masturbation or oral sex.

The Bible does not speak about either of these latter practices — at least not specifically. Of course it refers to the question of lust and improper sexual desires/activities, and general principles can be applied. It may seem that these sexual alternatives are better — or the lesser of the evils. Isn't it better, so the argument goes, for a girl to stimulate her boy-friend to climax with her hand than to do 'it' (sexual intercourse)?

The difficulty even here is that it makes the boy out to be some kind of monster who cannot control himself, and the girl to be avoiding problems by 'slaking his lust'. Is that the way Christians want to see themselves?

Similarly kissing may spread from the lips to the face to other parts of the body, until girl and boy are kissing each others genitals. This is what is called oral sex. Both partners may be stimulated to orgasm by sucking of the boy's penis or the girl's clitoris. Again the argument is that this is not technically intercourse. However the sensation and the experience are very much like intercourse; and leave the same troubling concerns of guilt and regret.

Are these practices to be seen as a help? They may be preventing what is seen as a worse situation, but this does not make them good. If you are doing it just because your boyfriend demands it, what does this say about your relationship, not only now, but in the future? Then again, if you are saying you want this satisfaction, and you have to have it, what does this say about you and your demands too?

What about the basic nature of God's love — loving one another in the same way as He loves us? When we say we want this kind of sex, are we talking about true love, or selfish gratification? What kind of love says, 'I want this, never mind what you think'? How do these acts affect our spiritual relationship?

God does not condemn us, but He does want us to experience more than some quick stimulation 'to take care of a problem'. To see sex in this way is to make it just a biological urge that needs satisfaction rather than a great gift of pleasure in love that you give to your beloved. Above all else, sex becomes self-centred instead of self-denying, taking rather

SOME SEXUAL ONELINERS

What thoughts are behind these statements. Write them right underneath so you can see exactly the kind of pressure that is being used. Then write down how you would answer. The first example shows you how:

Everybody else is doing it.
So you should too, or people will think you're odd. Peer pressure.
'I don't know what everybody else is doing. But I don't follow the crowds. I live my own life and make my own decisions. And if you really love me and say I'm so special, you would respect my decisions.'

But you know that I love you.

I need to see how much you love me.

I have needs too, you know.

Then you'll be a real woman.

We're going to get married anyway, aren't we?

I can't see that it's wrong for us.

I want to show you how much I love you.

Only we will know, anyway.

We need to find out if we're compatible.

than giving, seeking your own pleasure rather than thinking of the needs of the one you claim to love.

On a practical note, do remember that sexually-transmitted diseases can be passed on through oral sex (gonorrhoea for example). Also be aware that semen can enter the vagina even when spilt outside, and a baby can be conceived without the penis ever entering the vagina.

KEEPING IT GOOD

To go home without regrets is surely a great blessing in any relationship. Crying over 'going too far'; doubts as to whether what you're doing is right; worrying every month if your period is going to come — all these are aspects of a relationship that will not be remembered with joy. You are trying to build a solid base for the future, and playing around with sex will not help.

So avoid it! Sounds silly, and obvious — but you can. While it's normal to want to be alone with your boy-friend, don't choose bedrooms, parked cars — or late night sessions on couches. You can be alone in public places — countryside, parks, streets, restaurants . . . .

You want to talk — use a phone. Your parents may panic over phone bills, but if it avoids illicit sex, it's a price worth paying. Or write a letter; sometimes you can put your thoughts and ideas and principles better on paper.

He touches you more than you want. Tell him. Slap his hand down if you have to. That's more loving than letting the situation get out of control. Once you're down the route of heavy petting, then reverse gear is hard to find. Why? Because the body responds to stimulation by preparing for intercourse. It may not be your intention, but that's what happens inside. Stroking and caressing your breasts causes your nipples to swell and become extra-sensitive. At the same time the vagina secretes a lubrication that assists during intercourse. You feel hot and tingly all over. Your body prepares for sex.

Similarly your boy-friend. Touch, especially of the genitals, makes the penis stiff and sensitive. Again, his body prepares for sex.

Then suddenly you realize that you have to stop. The pleasant feelings that led you this far have to be thrown away, and you separate in a flurry of mixed emotions. Or . . . .

Heavy petting like this cannot help your decision not to become sexually involved, so realize this and don't start down the path. If you don't plan to go this particular direction, don't!

Remember: You only choose to lose control.

SELF-STIMULATION

Another difficulty is masturbation — when you stimulate yourself sexually, by fondling the genitals, and in girls particularly the clitoris. In one survey, 56 per cent of single female Christians admitted to

You want to talk — use the phone!

masturbation, and 89 per cent felt guilty about it. (Of single male Christians, 94 per cent admitted to masturbation, and 90 per cent felt guilty about it.)

What's thought to be wrong with it?

In the past some strange beliefs were held. Masturbation was said to be responsible for insanity and epileptic fits, blindness and infertility. Such ideas were obviously designed as a means to try and prevent what was seen as a perverted and filthy act.

Today the opposite extreme has been reached: if it feels good, do it. It won't hurt you — everybody's doing it.

But for the Christian? We need to go beyond the right or wrong stage and understand. Most children play with their genitals. Many teenagers masturbate, with apparently no ill effects then or later in marriage. Some men claim to masturbate simply to remove the tension that accompanies the build up of semen (that would normally be lost through nocturnal emissions, or 'wet dreams'), and that this is not an erotic act. If masturbation is simply an alleviation of tension then any moral questions would not be asked.

However, masturbation has at its heart a particular flaw — it can be seen as an expression of self-love. Masturbation has been called 'solo sex'. We must be careful not to condemn, for nowhere does the Bible speak against masturbation. However, the Bible is clear in identifying sex as being designed for two people (of the opposite sex)! In masturbation you seek your own pleasure, in making love you seek the other's pleasure — which in the end means greater pleasure for both.

Also, masturbation can become obsessive, especially for some (particularly men). In some cases, a person's whole life can revolve around their times of masturbation and their particular fantasies. Masturbation can also be addictive, for having discovered a way of pleasing yourself, you want to repeat the experience. In some cases this may mean excessive time spent on masturbating. No one would agree that this was a healthy state in which to live, and external treatment and counselling may be necessary.

Lastly, it is possible that masturbation may prevent the development of right relationships with the other sex. If you can turn yourself on, why do you need anyone else? For the stimulation you receive from someone else may not be quite what you like, having discovered what you enjoy. Masturbation may complicate your relationships, and can affect sexual behaviour within subsequent marriage. One girl admitted that when she masturbated she had a vision of sex with a perfect man. She also admitted that any actual man would have difficulty meeting the expectations of her fantasy.

DEALING WITH MASTURBATION

In dealing with problems of masturbation, you need to determine in your mind whether you are feeling guilty over the action, or over sex itself. All too often there is a confusion here which leads to even more problems. To focus in on masturbation as a major problem may even make the situation worse (which is why parents need to be very careful in how they speak to children on this subject). Remember sex is not dirty. Your masturbatory fantasies may be a problem and cause you very real guilt, but do not assume that all sex is, therefore, bad. For if this does happen, it tends to confirm the habit of masturbation as a way of relieving the tension.

The usual advice of taking a cold shower doesn't do the issue justice. Over-exercise (through sports, for example) is sometimes recommended, reasoning that you will be too tired to masturbate. Yet when you are tired is often when it is easier to follow a habit.

A few suggestions:

▶ Replace the fantasy. Often masturbation is associated with fantasy images you play with in your brain. *You* are the one who chooses the images, so choose ones that may be sensory but not sexual.

▶ Occupy your mind, without worrying. Make sure you have plenty to do, and if masturbation is a late night thing, take some other activity to bed — reading, craft work, even calculating your personal finances!

▶ Discover others. Masturbation is frequently a symptom of loneliness — a way to satisfy your own longings for intimacy. This is not saying 'get a boy-friend' and everything will be OK — rather be involved with *people* — whoever. Don't look to yourself to supplying your emotional needs — this is self-centred and soul-destroying.

▶ Avoid situations and materials that arouse you. Don't feed your mind fantasy images or sexual thoughts.

▶ Channel your mind into more productive activity, and make your own decisions about what you will and will not do. Be aware that often progress is slow, and do not feel defeated at failure. Finally, be aware that most people graduate from masturbation to a happy sexual relationship in marriage. (Though you shouldn't be looking to marriage as a cure!)

A MORE EXCELLENT WAY . . .

Paul in his great love chapter (1 Corinthians 13) speaks of a more excellent way. And that certainly

Keep your mind busy, do something that you can get involved in rather than laze about letting your thoughts wander.

made us, who wired us up to experience great physical pleasure and wonderfully intimate love, can rewire us and remake us. 'If anyone is in Christ, (s)he is a new creation; the

> **If you love, you will suffer, and if you do not love, you do not know the meaning of a Christian life.**
> AGATHA CHRISTIE

old has gone, the new has come!' (2 Corinthians 5:17, NIV, modified.) We are now 'born of God' and 'we may live a new life'. (John 1:13; Romans 6:4, NIV.)

So go back to God, share your deepest thoughts and feelings, your pain and guilt with Him. He will give you rest — and the strength to master your sexual drives as He remakes you in His image.

God's forgiveness is available to anyone. He will give you a new start where you can enjoy life again and find peace in yourself.

applies to sex! After reading this chapter, despair and discouragement can come rushing in as you see that all is not right, and that you've still got problems to solve.

But the assurance is that we don't fight these alone. The God who

QUESTIONS AND ANSWERS

What does oral sex mean? What about oral sex before marriage? It isn't really intercourse, is it? What is the Christian's view on oral sex? What do you think about oral sex?

The most frequently asked questions in the seminars we've conducted have been about oral sex. Oral sex is very much part of popular culture, as if it's just been invented! Christians have been divided over the rights and wrongs of oral sex. The Bible does not explicitly forbid or condone the practice, (it certainly doesn't say it is immoral or unnatural) so it is unwise to be dogmatic either way. From the statistics it would seem that most couples practise oral sex in marriage. This may also occur before marriage. The main worry is if this particular practice becomes the predominant means of sexual expression. Almost any form of sexual behaviour can become obsessive. If oral sex has been frequently practised before marriage (as a way of avoiding 'going all the way'), then it may be a problem for a good sexual relationship in married life. For whatever you may think, as an experience oral sex to orgasm is close to vaginal intercourse. Oral sex is still sex!

Why does the church say premarital sex is wrong? Isn't that just part of the way people used to be controlled by society?

Don't believe all that nonsense that says the church is just an agent of social control, and so all its beliefs should be abandoned. While the church may not have always acted from pure motives, the idea that teachings against premarital sex are just ways of promoting control is dangerous foolishness. The reason premarital sex is wrong is because of the damage is does, not primarily to society, but to you and your sexual partner(s).

I used to have sex with my boy-friends but now I have stopped all that. My current boy-friend doesn't see why I should deny him, though. What can I tell him to explain how I feel?

Hard question, and sad too. Learning late is better than not learning at all, and if your mistakes have taught you something, then all is not lost. But it's hard for others to see that, and we feel for your situation. Your current boy-friend (you don't say if he's a Christian or not) expresses a typical reaction: 'You're not a virgin, anyway.' But you must be true to your decisions, to what you believe, and to your own self-identity. By your words and actions you must show him how important this is *for you as a person* and that you're not just being awkward or strange as far as he is concerned. Share your ideas of God with him too, and pray that he will understand your need to be right with God — the fundamental desire of a Christian — not just in a 'not guilty' sense, but as a loved and trusted friend.

I tend to fondle myself, I think it is called 'manstribretion'. I cannot see where in the Bible it says it is wrong.
What does the Bible say about masturbation?

Two questions that reflect a great area of concern. That one of you should misspell the word illustrates the interest, but the difficulty about speaking openly on this subject. Again the Bible is silent on this specific practice. Yet solo sex is surely far from the ideal God intended, of two *making love* together. Did God make us with sexual drives that we should take care of ourselves? Although masturbation is very common (more among boys than girls), is viewed by many authorities as part of growing up, and is accepted as not making you blind or diseased as some scare tactics used to suggest, don't follow the way of the world and think it's good practice. While it may be true that you can't get pregnant from masturbating, it may only serve to increase your sexual frustration and lead to other areas of difficulty.

DEALING WITH THE FICTION

Here's some common fiction about sex. These wrong ideas often get in the way of a healthy relationship. Or they may lead you to make mistakes. So read them, and add your own comments to ours:

GETTING PREGNANT
You can't get pregnant if you have sex standing up.
Gravity isn't that powerful! You can get pregnant whatever position you use.
You can't get pregnant if you urinate after having sex.
Urine comes out through the urethra, not down through the vagina. So it doesn't 'wash out the sperms'. Nor do any other washes or douches provide an answer, because the sperms may have already passed up through the vagina.
You can't get pregnant if you have your period.
It is still possible, since periods can be irregular, and sperm can live inside your body for several days.
You can't get pregnant the first time you have sex.
Yes you can. Ask those who have.
You can't get pregnant if the man pulls out before ejaculating.
Sometimes semen can leak out before ejaculation. And sperm ejaculated anywhere near the vagina can swim in.

BOYS AND SEX
Boys need sex more than girls.
That kind of excuse is a sad comment on the male species! While it may seem that boys are more easily excited, to believe that they *must* have sex is foolish.
It's the girl's job to say 'No'.
Why should you bear the whole responsibility? You need to decide to say 'No' together.

Is it wrong to use appliances in order to get satisfaction, for instance, a vibrator?

Using a vibrator is another variation of masturbation, and the same thoughts apply. Once again it is 'solo sex' and as such is not fulfilling the ideal.

How does God feel about me now that I've done it?

This question was asked during a counselling session and shows the thought that 'Now God has to treat me as a real sinner.' Of course you need to take the situation seriously. Premarital sex cannot be termed a 'good idea'. But don't make the opposite mistake and think that this is the unforgivable sin, and that God shuts His face from you. You need to reject the idea that since you've done something wrong God can't help you. In fact you need God now more than ever. Tell Him exactly what you think and feel, ask for His forgiveness and accept the gracious mercy only He can give. And as Jesus said, 'Go and sin no more'!

If a girl teases a boy, she deserves what she gets.
Nothing that a girl does is any excuse for sex by force. Girls do need to avoid over-exciting behaviour, but should never believe that they have to give into any demands for sex.

If you don't give the boy what he wants, you won't have a boy-friend.
This can be argued both ways. If you do give him what he wants, he may then drop you. And if you don't, he may well respect you more. And if he doesn't respect you, did you really want him anyway?

The longer you spend with a boy, the more likely he is to demand sex.
Depends on the boy. It *isn't* true that men just want one thing. And it does depend on what you are doing together. If you spend a long time kissing and petting, the more likely you are to end up having sexual intercourse.

LOVE

If you don't have sex before marriage, you can't really be in love.
Or you are frigid, or a lesbian or whatever. These are just threats to force you into sex.

If you're really in love then nothing else matters.
So you have sex. And you get a disease. Or you feel guilty. Or you end up hating yourself. Love is the opposite — you don't put the other person at risk — you want the very best for him or her. So if you really do love, then everything does matter.

If you have sex with your boy-friend, you will love each other more.
Or less. Sex can also destroy a relationship, and to have sex is no way to guarantee greater love — unless you have made that total commitment for life by getting married.

If you have sex before you get married, you'll know if you're compatible.
The statistics show otherwise. Instead of making sure, you often end up with comparisons with other sexual partners. And once you have had sex together, can you back away from it so easily?

9

Broken sex?

The acts of the sinful nature are obvious: sexual immorality, impurity and debauchery . . . . Galatians 5:19, NIV.

FACTORS OF BROKENNESS

When you think of the beauty that God placed in our sexuality, it's terribly sad to realize how far we have gone in twisting, tearing and destroying God's great gift. All too often, all that's left is what we call 'broken sex'. Perverted and corrupted, modern sexual expression is almost always far from God's ideal.

Like a diet of bad news, the wars and murders and famines and the rest: to concentrate on our sexual brokenness can hurt us further. Only read here what you really need to know. The gloss the Devil puts on his perversions soon tarnishes, and leaves you with a handful of dust instead of living blessings. So remember: whatsoever things are good . . . think on these things!

But just as the medical handbook has to illustraste disease and sickness in order to demonstrate the cure, we'll look briefly as some factors of brokenness.

ADULTERY: ITS REAL MEANING

How sad it must have been for God to have had to include 'You shall not commit adultery' in the ten commandments. The fact that He had to do so suggests it was a definite problem among His people — and it still is.

Again, this is not God being anti-sex. It simply reflects the wisdom of God in knowing that, like a worm in the bud, sexual activity outside of marriage is highly destructive. It breeds secrecy and dishonesty, it encourages mistreatment of others and self-centredness. And tragically, adultery is so often portrayed as being the norm, acceptable, 'a good thing'.

What the fiction-writers *don't* mention of course is the down-side of fractured relationships. The tearing apart of what God put together,

---

SEX The exchange of two momentary desires and the contact of two skins.
NICOLAS CHAMFORT

the 'tug-of-love' over the children, the breakup of the home, the distressing dislocation of life, school, work — everything. We know — we've seen it so often. Even 'in the church', where the statistics are not so different from society's, one in three marriages ends in divorce. The statistics of millions of divorces only mirror the terrible tragedies of shattered dreams and devastated hopes.

The personal search for self-fulfilment, to 'do your own thing', usually means in practice that everybody else can be got rid of — even husbands and wives. Such ideas fail to see that trust once broken is so hard to mend. Second marriages (and third, and fourth, and so on!) are much more likely to fail, and the reason is obvious: marriage is a temporary situation that can be altered at your convenience.

Selfishness is at the centre of sex for many people today. Wanting 'something better' leads you to look for 'greener grass'. And so you start looking, and you find. Just like David and Bathsheba. Just one look — that's all it took. One look that was dwelt upon, a scene that was replayed, the opening screen in an imagined relationship that David then made real.

It seemed like fun. A beautiful woman attracts David. Bathsheba is flattered by the King's attention. But what a bitter result — and there are *always* consequences, even if no one ever finds out.

As you read the sorry story in 2 Samuel 11, what begins as a 'romantic affair' soon degenerates into deception, plotting and eventually murder by remote control. Why? Because that's what illicit 'love' does. Such a clear illustration of the truth that sin kills — it is inherently self-destructive. Imagine the effect on the minds of the conspirators: David engineering a faithful friend's death; the widow weeping for a while before she moves in with David.

And then the ripping away of the veil of dishonesty by the prophet Nathan, the confronting of the immensity of the couple's sin. The results are not only for them, but for the whole society who see what their king has done. How far 'the Lord's anointed' had fallen! No wonder it was recorded, 'the thing David had done displeased the Lord.' (2 Samuel 11:27, NIV.)

And yet — yet there is a way back to God from the dark paths of sin. David bares his agonized soul as he writes Psalm 51. And in his confession and repentance we see the incredible graciousness of God. The consequences may still be bitter — but there is hope, there is repentance, there is salvation. We need to remember that. While adultery is a horrible offence that darkens the lives of all it touches, forgiveness (by God and the injured party) remains possible. And God — only God — can remake the guilty one: 'Create in me a pure heart, O

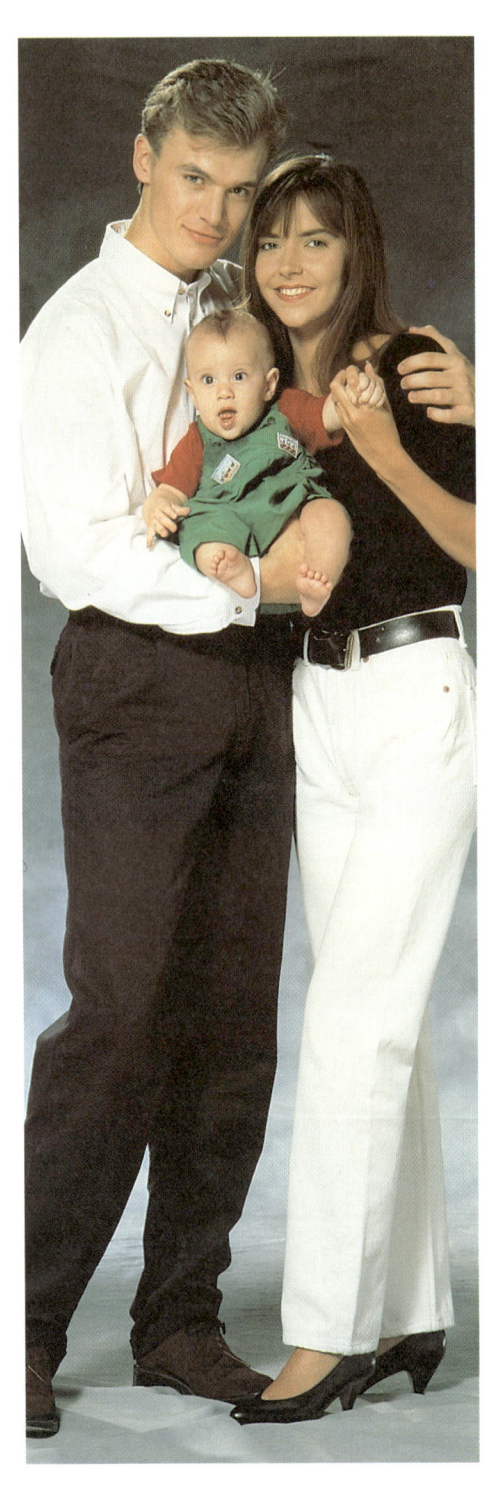

God, and renew a steadfast spirit within me. Do not cast me from your presence or take your Holy Spirit from me.' (Psalm 51:10, 11, NIV.)

And amazingly David and Bathsheba had a son, Solomon — blessed by God, despite the sins of his parents. But then again, think of how Solomon too became entrapped in sexual sins with his multiple wives and concubines . . . .

Adultery has consequences — even down the generations.

ABUSE: CHILDREN, WIVES, HUSBANDS, PARTNERS

Sexual abuse is any form of sexual activity carried out against another human being without their consent. It's estimated that one in four girls and one in eight boys have been sexually abused by the time they reach the adolescent years. The abuser is usually someone well known to the victim. Abuse can range from verbal attacks to physical assault, from improper behaviour to incest and rape.

Abuse is the great unmentionable that has scarred so many, and has stored up tragedy for years ahead. If you or someone known to you has experienced abuse, help is needed. While there have been difficulties caused by cases of 'false memories' and wrong accusations of sexual abuse by some, the subject still needs more openness and victims need much more assistance. Those who have been abused are also more

So many couples start off in a dream world only to find that romance becomes bitter and twisted by someone else breaking into their affections. Trust is broken and the relationship falls apart.

Waiting for mother or father who isn't coming home. Children are innocent victims of divorce and abuse, resulting in pain and long-term damage.

likely to abuse others when they grow up, so it's essential to break this cycle.

Despite all the agony and hurt, God is still there. And very often, only with a conviction of divine power can forgiveness be achieved and guilt erased. We know of one young woman abused in childhood by her father who has only recently been able to face the reality of her situation and experience healing and restoration. In her particular case this was made more difficult because her father was a church minister. You can imagine how this complicated her experience and made it even more distressing.

And yet she is now happily married, and sees the trauma of the past as something for which she was not responsible. All too frequently the victim blames himself or herself, believing they must have encouraged such mistreatment. The greatest abuse is of the position of love and trust as a parent or family member acting against one who is defenceless. The words of Jesus can be applied here: '"It would be better for him to be thrown into the sea with a millstone tied round his neck than for him to cause one of these little ones to sin."' (Luke 17:2, NIV.) And the little ones didn't sin anyway!

RAPE: SUPREME DESTRUCTIVE SELFISHNESS

If love is the highest expression of self-giving, then rape must be one of the worst expressions of selfishness. It is the violent taking without any thought for the other person. The rapist does not care about his victim as a human being.

You should also realize that rape has often little to do with sex, and much more with a desire to hurt, humiliate and denigrate. It is to have great power over the victim.

Rape is greatly under-reported. In the US there are probably more than a million cases of rape a year, yet only 20 per cent are reported. Many victims feel in some way responsible, or fear the publicity, or are intimidated into remaining silent. No one can force the issue, but not to report a rape has its own consequences — maybe for someone else.

If you are raped, do seek medical assistance at a hospital, and make sure you receive counselling both in any decisions you may make at the time, and later on.

One rape victim came to us for help. She was the daughter of a church minister. She refused to speak to anyone else, or be referred. Only we were to know.

She had left home for the first time as she began her university course. The rape occurred in the very first week, and was carried out by the person responsible for caring for the welfare and safety of students in the dormitory. Later investigation showed that he had also raped another new student, and that this had probably happened several times before.

Despite this, she would not make any report to the authorities, though she received medical attention from the local hospital after the rape.

Our main concern had to be for her welfare — and the following weeks were traumatic for the three of us. Her personality changed. She dressed in rough clothes, usually old jeans, as if she were making some statement about herself as being unattractive. Her attitudes became hard and cynical. Her course work suffered, and she developed an uncaring outlook on the world.

After a long time, she began to come to terms with the rape — that she had not been responsible, that she must not allow the rape to destroy her, that with God she could rebuild who she was. But it takes much time, and in some way the memory of that appalling night will always affect her.

And yet the rapist probably has no idea of what he did, and has probably forgotten already.

We still weep for the damage done to and the terrible consequences for a girl with bright hopes and an innocent smile. Remember that rape is most commonly carried out by someone known to the victim.

Date rape has risen alarmingly and needs to be mentioned. Make as sure as you can that you don't place yourself in a situation where date rape could occur, inform yourself about preventative measures, and report any incident. Most date rapes

Rape is the worst expression of selfishness. The rapist has no consideration for his victim yet the terrible consequences make her feel worthless, dirty and degraded.

have common factors: the boy was not known (and so his behaviour could not be predicted), the couple were alone for some time, and alcohol or drugs were involved. So avoid making yourself vulnerable to someone you don't know well, don't spend time alone, avoid parties, etc. where alcohol or drugs may be used.

The story of the rape of Tamar (recorded in 2 Samuel 13) is worth reading to understand some frequent aspects of rape. Firstly, Amnon became obsessed with his half-sister Tamar. He thought he was in love, but we would probably call this an obsessive infatuation. This might have come to nothing had Amnon not told his uncle about his feelings, and his uncle suggested a corrupt strategy. Following his uncle's plan, Amnon arranged to fake sickness, and have Tamar attend to him. When she refused his invitation to 'Come to bed' Amnon raped her. Note the exact words:

'But he would not listen to her; and since he was stronger than she was, he overpowered her and raped her. Then Amnon was filled with a deep hatred for her; he hated her now even more than he had loved her before. He said to her, "Get out!"' (2 Samuel 13:14, 15.)

Infatuation leads to lust. Lust leads to rape. Rape leads to hatred and rejection. A terrible catalogue of one disaster after another.

And the story doesn't end there. Tamar ended up living at her brother Absalom's house, 'sad and lonely'. And after two years Absalom took revenge on Amnon and had him killed. This in turn led to the estrangement of Absalom from his father David, which then led to . . .

See how actions have consequences? An infatuation that led to rape eventually caused many deaths and (along with other factors) nearly destroyed the whole kingdom when Absalom made war on his father David.

Obsession, madness, rejection, denial — familiar aspects of rape and violence in this perverted world.

PORNOGRAPHY: WHAT THIS IS AND WHAT IT DOES

'If the purpose of pornography is to excite sexual desire, it is unnecessary for the young, inconvenient for the middle aged and unseemly for the old.' *Malcolm Muggeridge*.

And yet pornography is widespread. A general definition is of any material — printed, pictures, video — that shows explicit sexual acts designed to cause sexual arousal.

From the magazines on the newsagent's top shelf to the videos in the rental store, from the cheap pulp novels to the sex shops downtown, pornography is easily available in many places around the world today.

Most women find pornography's appeal hard to understand. Pictures of naked men, or specific descriptions of the sex act do not normally arouse women. But it is important to realize the difference in the 'wiring' between the male and female, and that pornography has a profound effect on most men.

While in no way excusing pornography, the fact is that the male's sexual response is triggered by the naked female form. If this was all, then while reprehensible, pornography might be seen as some lesser evil. The deeper problem is that pornography involves the degradation of women, reinforces male domination, and is sometimes linked with violence.

What relationship is there between a man and a picture on a page? And what kind of concept of female identity is promoted by this? Perhaps worst of all, what is the man doing to himself by becoming 'object' orientated?

Pornography is undoubtedly damaging to the user, while he may not become a serial rapist. Why? Because porn misrepresents women and their sexuality, confirms immature male attitudes, and trivializes God's gift of a complete relationship, it can have no part in the life of a Christian. Any attempt to bring it into a relationship should be resisted.

PROSTITUTION

'Prostitutes and immoral women

are a deadly trap.' Proverbs 23:27. While the idea of payment for sex has a long and sad history, this practice is far from God's ideal of a long-lasting and fulfilled relationship between man and woman. The Bible consistently speaks against the principle of prostitution, because like all other forms of broken sex, it is a cheap substitute and in no way reflects the highest principles of self-giving in love. Rather it is a sordid contract of a moments pleasure in return for money. Like pornography, prostitution humiliates women, and turns them into sexual objects that are paid to perform on demand. As one prostitute once said, 'I might as well be a robot.' Turning people into things is part of the demonic plan to destroy human relationships.

For this reason Paul writes to the sexually lax members in Corinth: 'Shall I then take the members of Christ and unite them with a prostitute? Never! Do you not know that he who unites himself with a prostitute is one with her in body?' 1 Corinthians 6:15, 16, NIV.

Yet the Bible speaks compassionately of those women who, for various reasons, have become entrapped in prostitution. Jesus did not turn them away, and told the self-righteous religious leaders of His time: '"The tax collectors and the prostitutes are going into the Kingdom of God before you."' Matthew 21:31. Rahab the prostitute in Jericho is commended as an example of faith in Hebrews 11. This is not to condone prostitution; but Scripture realizes that often women are the victims themselves. Jesus showed that rescue and healing from broken sex is part of His offer of salvation.

SEX: THE PRINCIPLES BY WHICH CHRISTIANS SHOULD ACT

Sex is good.
GENESIS 2:18-25.

Sex has consequences.
GALATIANS 6:7, 8; ROMANS 1:24, 25.

Sex must not control you.
1 THESSALONIANS 4:4;
1 CORINTHIANS 6:12-14; 10:23, 24.

Sex is secondary to love.
1 CORINTHIANS 13:1-13.

Sex can sometimes only be handled by running.
GENESIS 39:12.

Sex becomes more dangerous as you mess around with it.
JAMES 1:12-15;
1 THESSALONIONS 4:3-8.

Sex is a great temptation, but it can be resisted.
1 CORINTHIANS 10:13.

Sex is two becoming one.
GENESIS 2:24; MATTHEW 19:5;
1 CORINTHIANS 6:16.

Sex must honour God.
1 CORINTHIANS 6:20.

Sex is designed to be the completion of intimacy.
GENESIS 2:23, 24.

SEXUAL PERVERSIONS: A DENIAL OF GOD

The capacity of the human mind to corrupt and deprave seems almost without limit. When God is ignored, even such pure and beautiful aspects of our lives as sexuality in love are turned into gross and disgusting acts that debase us even more. In the same way as when God looked at the people on the earth before the flood and 'saw how wicked everyone on earth was and how evil their thoughts were all the time' (Genesis 6:5), God must view our world in a very similar light. The preoccupation with sex — especially sex performed in animalistic and uncaring ways — shows how far humanity is from its God-intended ideal. 'The heart is deceitful above all things, and desperately wicked: who can know it?' Jeremiah 17:9, KJV.

How tragic for God to have to spell out to His people what really was perverted sex! What God says in Leviticus 18-20 (and elsewhere) about forbidden sexual relations should surely have been obvious, yet God is forced to be totally explicit — presumably because some of His people were actually doing (or might in the future do) such things.

Imagine how God must have felt to say: 'Do not have sex with your mother, or sister, or granddaughter.' Or, 'Do not make your daughter a prostitute.' Or, 'Do not have sex with another man.'

Or 'Do not have sex with an animal.' And God has to be even more explicit on the last perversion,

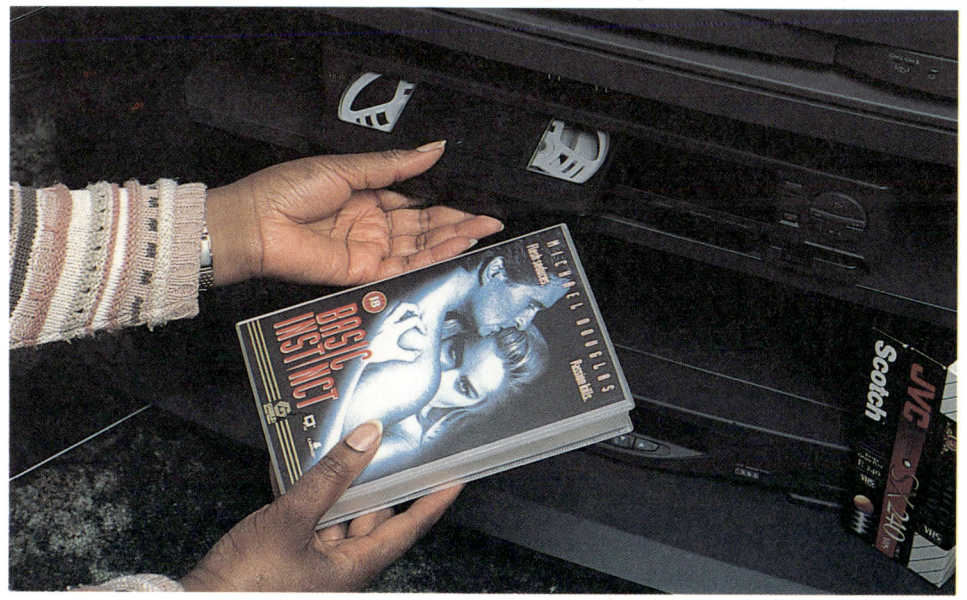

Videos are a widely available means of sexual exploitation. Undoubtedly damaging to watch, they destroy relationships and degrade a woman to the position of being a sex object.

spelling out that this applies to women too.

Such kinds of sexual perversions were punishable by death, and show just how seriously God took the abuse of sex. To engage in such practices did not only debase and degrade the individual, but would affect others, and eventually the whole society — as happened with Sodom and Gomorrah. Ultimately sexual perversions are anti-God in their results, since they twist and corrupt the heart of true and loving relationships.

Enough said. Just one final point — the perversions described above are clearly condemned in the Bible. Sometimes people believe that other acts are perversions, even some that would seem to others to be quite inoffensive such as different positions during intercourse. What God has not spoken about must be left to the conscience and the unselfish loving relationship between man and wife.

HOMOSEXUALITY

'The love that previously dared not speak its name has now grown hoarse from screaming it.' (Robert Brustein, *New York Times*, 22 November 1977.)

The modern acceptance of homosexuality as an equally valid form of sexuality is at odds with God's clear position in Scripture: '"Do not lie with a man as one lies with a woman; that is detestable."' Leviticus 18:22, NIV. "'If a man lies with a man as one lies with a woman, both of them have done what is detestable. They must be put to death; their blood will be on their own heads."' Leviticus 20:13, NIV.

No amount of rationalizing changes the fact that homosexuality is part of broken sex; a defective and distorted form of sex. Like the other forms of broken sex mentioned above, that does not mean to say God has given up on homosexuals. It is not the person, but the practice of perversions that leads to self-destruction and the debasement of others that God is so much against.

Much modern research has been directed at identifying the cause of homosexuality. Hormone irregularities during pregnancies, genetic abnormalities, lack of same sex parental love, and retarded emotional development have all been cited as factors; and there may be some truth in some of these assertions. It is certainly true that many adolescents form an attachment to a member of the same sex as they develop physically and emotionally. And with the emphasis on homosexuality today, some believe that having such an experience makes them gay. This is a false conclusion.

However, to say, 'I'm gay because God made me that way', is to deny God's clearly stated attitude towards homosexuality, and to refuse His offer of healing and change. The Christian church in the corrupt heart of the Empire of Rome had battles to fight along these lines, and it is important to note the connection

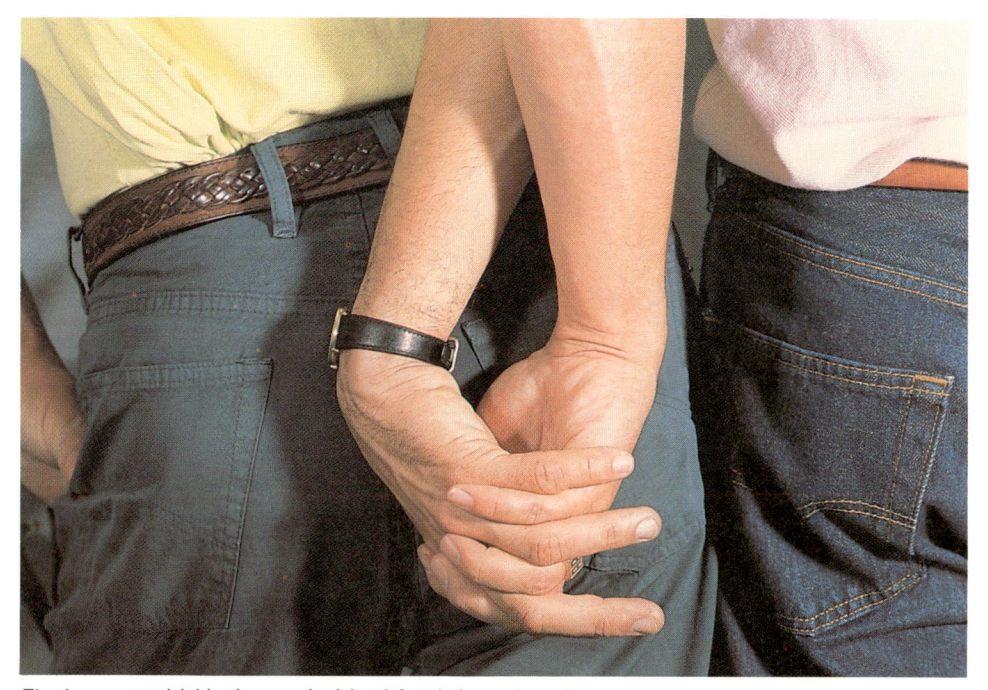

The homosexual lobby has pushed hard for their version of sexuality to be accepted as normal human behaviour, but no way can it be seen as a natural relationship, it's a defective and distorted form of sex.

between broken sex (including homosexuality), idolatry and the rejection of the true Creator God:

'They exchanged the truth of God for a lie, and worshipped and served created things rather than the Creator — who is forever praised. Amen. Because of this, God gave them over to shameful lusts. Even their women exchanged natural relations for unnatural ones. In the same way the men also abandoned natural relations with women and were inflamed with lust for one another. Men committed indecent acts with other men, and received . . . the due penalty for their perversion.' Romans 1:25-27, NIV.

Once again broken sex is destructive to the whole life-style, to the very existence of humanity itself. The ugly nature of such perversion is shown in the state of the towns of Sodom and Gomorrah, which eventually needed to be destroyed in order to stop the plague spreading.

Lest it be said that homosexuality is unfairly targeted, note the all-inclusive list of broken sex that will prevent salvation, unless conversion comes: 'Neither the sexually immoral nor idolaters nor adulterers nor male prostitutes nor homosexual offenders . . . will inherit the kingdom of God.' 1 Corinthians 6:9, 11, NIV.

This sad chapter describes the way we have (often intentionally) damaged God's great gift of sexuality and reflects our own selfish sinfulness. Broken sex is just another demonstration of how far we have gone away from God and His ideals for His children. For Christians it demands attention in the way we relate to others whose lives have been blighted with such broken attitudes to sex. We need to think how we can share God's good news of salvation from these sexual sins and others. We must consider how we can rebuild our sexual brokenness and experience the healing and restoration of true, honest, pure and wholesome sex in our own lives.

I FEEL SO GUILTY

Sometimes our feelings can be damaging too. We need to deal with them. And they are not always right, either. So look at each of these true statements, and see how much they apply to you.

▶ No life is so badly messed up that God cannot fix it. He may not be able to take away all the consequences of your sins, but you have the assurance of His forgiveness and spiritual healing.

▶ While you cannot get your virginity back, you don't have to keep on sinning! Don't feel you have no chance to come back to God.

▶ As Jesus said to the woman taken in adultery — neither do I condemn you. Go and sin no more. God is not in the business of condemning people — He just wants them to leave their lives of sin and come to Him.

▶ If you were not the one responsible, *then you are not guilty for what happened*.

The Christian when relating to those abused by bad sex habits must be motivated by care and concern.

QUESTIONS AND ANSWERS

What causes homosexuality? How can there be homosexuals inside the church? What makes someone homosexual?

Questions like these are frequently asked during relationship seminars. From both sides a curiosity exists as to why someone should prefer a member of his or her own sex as a sexual partner. On the matter of causes much debate rages, since a great deal is at stake. If you're made that way, if you can't help yourself, then homosexuality can then be accepted as part of your genetic make-up. And some research has tried to support this thesis, though much is now discredited.

Other studies point to homosexuality as behaviour that is learned. Like any other learnt behaviour it is capable of change. From the biblical perspective this must be the position to take. For while some may be more inclined to homosexuality than others, as an actual behaviour it is acquired through learning and experiment. Like any other deviation from God's original plan for human sexuality, homosexual behaviour can be changed. There is a way back to God's pattern for human sexuality.

As for homosexuals in the church, you may as well ask about other forms of 'broken sex'. Perhaps homosexuality bothers Christians more than other sexual behaviour, but sinners in the church are not unusual. What is unacceptable is to suggest that it's OK to be a Christian homosexual, and actively to pursue that kind of life-style. The Bible's position must be maintained, and it doesn't help for sin to be considered acceptable.

What is 'normal' sex?

A loaded question! For to say that you can't define what exactly is 'normal' might imply to some that any sexual activity is acceptable. And to say that 'normal' sex is what 'I personally prefer' can exclude other sexual actions that may be perfectly OK. However, enough evidence exists to describe what is commonly understood to be 'normal' — if by 'normal' you mean practised by the majority (and the majority is not always right!). Majority-practised sex includes sexual foreplay (kissing, cuddling, petting), mutual stimulation (by hand contact), genital intercourse, and oral sex. Where Christians certainly disagree with the majority is *when* all this is to occur — sexual intercourse only within marriage.

If a Christian woman is raped, and becomes pregnant, is an abortion acceptable? If not, why not?

Abortion in extreme circumstances poses a dilemma for all concerned. Certainly there is no place for abortion on demand as a general procedure for unwanted pregnancies, as a so-called 'method of contraception'. However, in the case of certain genetic conditions (if the foetus will die before birth anyway as, for example, when the growing baby has no brain) then a strong case may be made for abortion. In the case of pregnancy as a result of rape, many conflicting emotions may arise. Hasn't the woman the right to determine what happens in her own body? Why should she be sentenced to relive that rape every time she looks at that child so conceived? This pregnancy was forced on her, so she should be able choose to terminate it. So run the pro-abortion arguments. On the other hand, why should an innocent child have to pay the price for someone else's crime? Is it right for innocent life to be terminated? What about the rights of the growing baby? We believe that where God has not specifically spoken, and bearing in mind all the possible complications that such a situation can bring, none of us has the right to decide for someone else in such a terrible situation.

If you suffer from sexual frustration is it OK to get relief from porno magazines?

This question probably came from one of the guys. However, we've included it here for two reasons:

1. A few girls develop a similar kind of interest in pornography that guys do.

2. You need to see from 'the other side of the fence' too.

You ask if it's 'OK to get relief'. If your sexual needs drive you to this, then we are truly sorry for your experience. But we wonder if you can blame your sexual frustration alone — are you such a slave to your passions? Or is it a convenient excuse? On top of that, you're programming your mind to a particularly offensive view of human sexuality in viewing pornography. The best definition of the difference between love and lust is that love looks to pleasing the lover, while lust only thinks of satisfying self. Pornography doesn't leave you undamaged; it leads you to think of sex as purely an act, images of objects that gratify your cravings. Perhaps that's the worst thing about pornography; it reduces your ability to love truly and be loved in a fulfilled sexual experience. No, it's not OK.

Why do men go to prostitutes?

Most of the reasons are more like excuses. It may be that they have some particular desire or fantasy that cannot be part of their sexual relationship with their partner, if they have one. For others it is a poor substitute for a relationship with women that they do not have. We would guess for most it is simply for sexual satisfaction, whether they are married or not. Ultimately it is because of sin and evil, the corrupting of sex into something that is bought and sold like some cattle market. Tragic.

Why do you think adultery is so bad?

Look again at David and Bathsheba. Their lust did not only affect them, but it led to lies and deceit, the arranged murder of Bathsheba's husband, and a breakdown in respect for the

Devastation, broken self-esteem and guilt, are the painful results of adultery.

monarchy (and God too). David and Bathsheba's actions, resulting in a damaged view of what was acceptable, had an impact throughout the country. For if the king can do it.... Adultery *always* has an impact, even if no one else knows about it. The broken self-esteem, the hidden guilt, the painful complicating of nearly every aspect of life — these are not considered in the heat of the moment, but they necessarily will and do come to haunt the adulterers. Most of all, adultery is a betrayal of trust, and a trust that reflects not only on your marriage partner, but on God too. For faith is trust in God, and if you break trust in any area of life, you compromise your trusting relationship to God. No wonder God used adultery as a picture to describe how He felt when betrayed by His children, Israel. Ultimately, *that's* why adultery is so bad.

If a Christian woman is being physically abused by a non-Christian husband, does she have to stay with him?

Some have read Paul's statements (for example 1 Corinthians 7:10-14) to mean that a Christian woman should stay with her husband, no matter what. Not, we believe, a true understanding, nor the way the God of grace operates. Physical abuse does not have to be tolerated by any, Christian or not. And if children are involved, to see such violence (and experience it too) is extremely damaging to their own personalities. The situation must be resolved quickly, either by making sure the abuse stops, or by parting company. Divorce does not necessarily have to be contemplated, but separation from an abusive husband is essential.

10

WARNING! sex can seriously damage your health

Evil desire conceives and gives birth to sin; and sin, when it is full-grown, gives birth to death. James 1:15.

Sex can seriously damage your health. In fact it can kill you. So dangerous is casual sex that it should carry a mandatory health warning. While the sexually-transmitted diseases (STDs) mentioned here will obviously only relate to those who are sexually active, the information must be part of decisions about sex, now and in the future.

For in the foolish passion of infatuation or the mistaken identification of sex for love are many hidden dangers that the glamorizers of sex don't tell you about.

If you'd seen
▶ women weeping because of diseases that have deprived them of the joy of having babies
▶ men in agonies of guilt as to how they can explain their infection to their new girl-friend
▶ the newly-married couple torn apart by some legacy from the past

THEN — you would think twice about the 'fun' of casual sex . . .

That's not to intimidate or scare. We just need to be realistic, and acknowledge the scale of the problem. Some sexually-transmitted diseases (formerly called venereal diseases) have become much more widespread, despite better medical treatment, due to increased sexual activity. The risk of acquiring some form of infection, especially from someone whose background is unknown to you, is significant enough for you to be seriously concerned. The tragedy is that it only takes one foolish act to become infected — perhaps with even a fatal infection.

The question, 'Is it worth the risk?', is a valid one, despite what the promoters of 'sex is just for fun' may say. So let's examine some of the facts about sexually-transmitted diseases.

DISEASES: THE PHYSICAL SYMPTOMS

Probably the most common form of sexually-transmitted disease is gonorrhoea, which is caused by a bacterium. Infection in women can often go unnoticed until it is well developed, at which time symptoms may include a discharge from the vagina, pain during urination, genital irritation and unusually heavy periods. If the disease is not treated (usually by penicillin and other kinds of antibiotics) it can cause inflammation of the pelvis which is a common cause of infertility.

Genital herpes is caused by a virus (herpes simplex I and II). Simplex I is responsible for cold sores, and therefore is one kind of STD that can be spread other than by penis-vaginal intercourse, since oral-genital contact by someone with cold sores can transmit the virus to their partner. Oral sex by someone who has cold sores is, therefore, very irresponsible. Genital herpes shows itself in small painful blisters on the genitals, and may be accompanied by fever and headaches. The virus may remain dormant for long periods, or may be responsible for many breakouts. Babies are at particular risk if the mother has a breakout at birth, and some research indicates that herpes leads to a higher risk of cervical cancer. There is no cure for genital herpes, though the symptoms can be alleviated by medical treatment.

Genital warts are also caused by a virus, and may be removed in the same way as other warts. Again genital cancer risk appears to be higher with those who have had genital warts.

Chlamydia is another bacterial infection that can have similar results in women as gonorrhoea, as well as causing complications during pregnancy. It is not treatable by penicillin, so other antibiotic treatments are used.

AIDS is caused by the human immunodeficiency virus for which there is no cure. The virus is transmitted through bodily fluids, most importantly in semen, sexual secretions and blood. Despite the emphasis on 'safe sex' the only safe way to avoid this infection is avoid all possibility of the transfer of bodily fluids. Even condoms do not provide total protection, though they do reduce the risk. Not everyone infected by the virus develops AIDS immediately, however it is thought that everyone who is HIV positive will eventually develop AIDS.

AIDS The sinister killer

AIDS is no joke. For whatever you've heard about it, the truth is probably worse. This invisible killer is hard to detect, and destroys by leaving its victims open to all kind of diseases.

Let us spell it out for you. For many people, AIDS is something other people get. And they think they cannot catch AIDS because they only sleep with 'clean' partners.

Listen. AIDS isn't to do with cleanliness. You cannot see AIDS. You need a very powerful microscope to see this tiny virus. The most attractive human beings may have AIDS. And you don't have to sleep around to catch AIDS — one act of sexual intercourse with an infected partner can be enough.

Where did AIDS come from? It may have its origins in certain kinds of monkeys. What is more important to know is how it spreads and what it does. The HIV virus responsible for AIDS spreads through infected body fluids such as blood and semen. The main way it spreads is through sexual intercourse, either homo- or hetero-sexual (same sex or different sex). Other ways include the sharing of needles by drug addicts (infected blood is spread from one user to another); blood transfusions (although this is much less common today now that people have become aware of the problem); and from mother to an unborn child.

How can it be stopped? By avoiding sex! (And by not sharing needles through illegal drug use, but that's another question.) The term 'safe sex' has been invented to encourage people to take care when they have sex. But even when condoms are used, there's still a 20 per cent risk of becoming infected by HIV.

Another way is to make sure your partner has had an AIDS test and that it is negative. However, due to the way the virus works, the test may be negative and still he can be infected with HIV. According to scientists, you can test negative for twelve months after becoming infected. This means that a negative test is no guarantee.

But there is *no chance* of being infected with HIV between husband and wife who have not indulged in sex before marriage and do not cheat on their partners. It cannot be caught through the air or from mosquitos or from unusual sexual positions. The very rare instances (like a dentist infecting his patients) are so unusual as to be notable, although a health worker should certainly not be practising in such a way.

What does this virus do? HIV works by slowly destroying the body's ability to defend itself against infections, and by causing other damage to this 'immune system'.

The result is that you are laid open to many other diseases, and once this stage of AIDS is reached then death is inevitable.

The time it takes from first infection with HIV to AIDS varies from eight months to several years (up to ten has been recorded). This means that a person may be infected for many years before they realize anything is wrong, and may have passed the virus on to many other people.

Once the virus has reduced this ability to fight infection, then the body is wide open to such attack.

Sixty per cent of AIDS sufferers contract pneumonia, and also suffer from other respiratory infections. Severe diarrhoea with weight loss is another common feature, as are other gastrointestinal problems. One organism that causes diarrhoea among travellers abroad has been found to kill AIDS patents. Infection by herpes at the anus is another very painful disease that may accompany AIDS.

Lymph glands may swell and become cancerous, many kinds of painful skin conditions can develop,

A greatly enlarged view of the AIDS virus attacking white blood cells. This means that eventually the body loses the ability to fight infection.

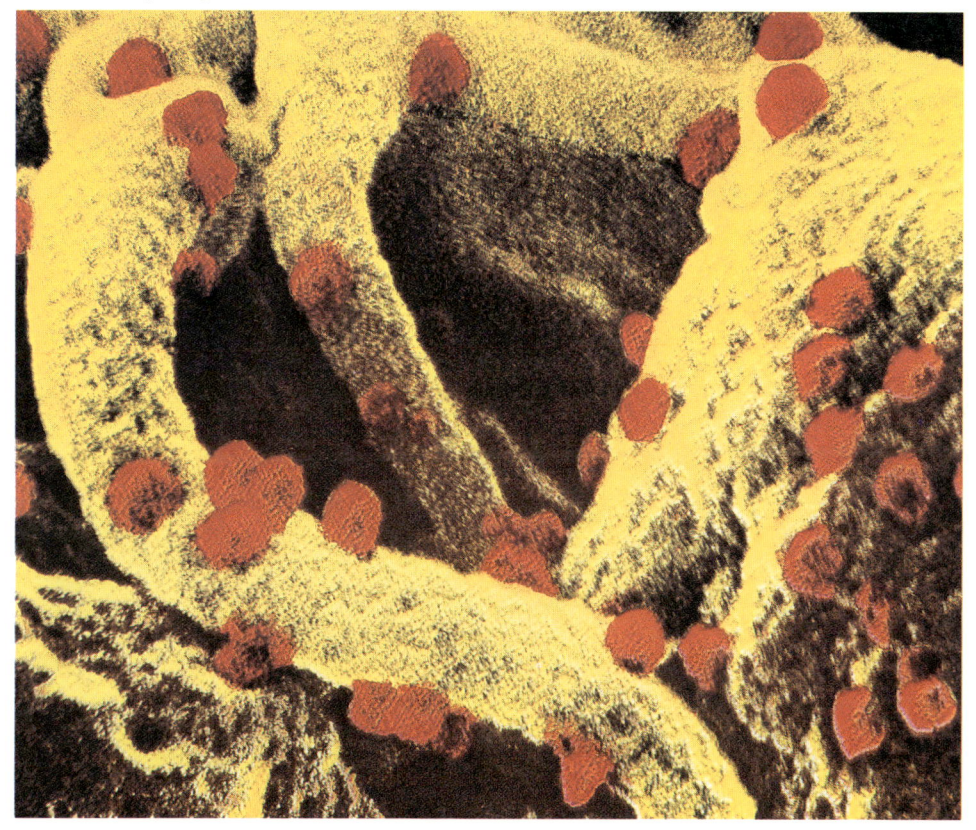

along with rapid ageing and the development of unusual cancers, in particular Kaposi's sarcoma.

All in all, AIDS leads to a terrible catalogue of illness and disease that may be extended. As many have noted, is it worth taking the risk in view of such terrible possible results?

If you're not yet convinced how appalling AIDS is, here is a summarized account of a woman who is HIV positive. Think how it affects everything about her life. And put yourself in her position.

'Grace' does not explain how she became infected with HIV, except to mention that neither she nor her husband were virgins when they married. She had been having repeated symptoms of flu for several months, and eventually her doctor had suggested having an AIDS test. She'd agreed, knowing that it would be negative since she was a Christian, didn't use drugs, wasn't a homosexual or a prostitute. But she tested positive.

Her husband left her, believing she had become infected by cheating on him. And she was pregnant.

The baby was born HIV positive, but after eighteen months she thankfully tested negative. However, Grace has had more frequent health problems including serious headaches, severe diarrhoea and cervical cancer. Sometimes, she says, she is so tired she can hardly get out of bed.

But she says the hardest part was

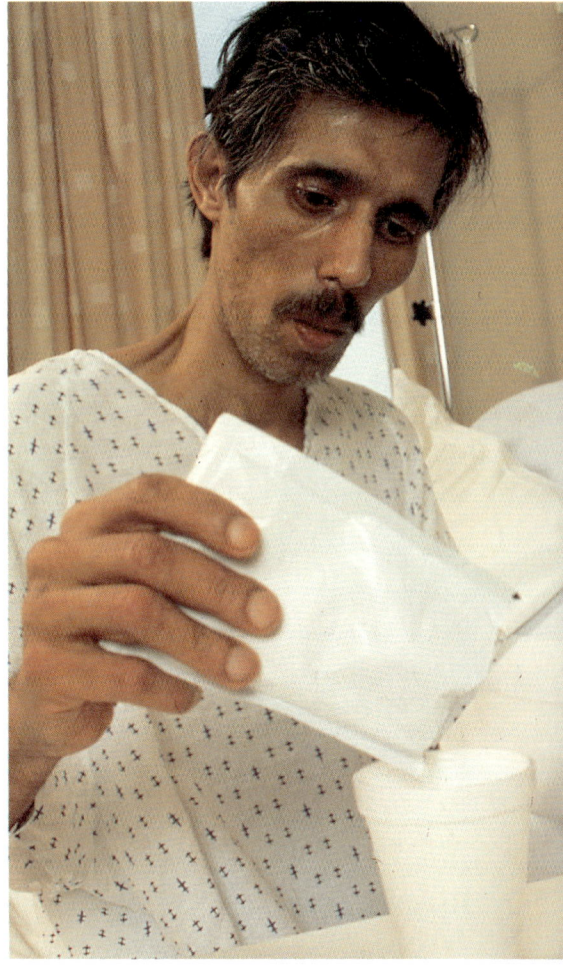

Although there has been intensive research into AIDS no long-term effective treatment has been found. It's still a killer.

dealing with HIV in connection with her faith and belief in God. She had expected God to take care of her. Was He now punishing her? And what about the others in her church family? Thankfully they have become supportive and helpful. She concludes by writing this: 'I know that my time on earth is limited, but these are the days I'll remember. I feel secure that my daughter will grow up in a church that cares about her even when she's wounded. I have glimpsed the tender, compassionate face of God, and I look forward to seeing Him face to face.'

A wonderful statement of faith, and of the help of a caring church. But how immensely tragic that Grace will not have the rich privilege of watching her daughter grow up, to know with a chilling certainty that her days are very limited. And for what? We're sure that she would not have traded that for all her life, and the pain of slowly dying as her little girl grows. And what of her daughter once she's gone?

The curse of AIDS goes far beyond the individual sufferer, as devastating as that may be. AIDS hurts all of us. And to be stopped, we all need to make the right choices, and not live like blind fools.

PRACTICAL CONSEQUENCES

It's easy to become almost paranoid after reading such a list of horrors! But do remember that unless someone has been infected in some other way (for example, at birth or through drug abuse) it is not possible for you or your partner to have any sexually-transmitted disease if you are both virgins. That is certainly one factor to bear in mind when answering the question, 'Why wait?'

Beyond that, it is also true that the more partners you or your boyfriend have had increases the risk, while the fewer the partners, the lower the risk. So it is important to discover from each other the level of previous sexual activity. Sometimes this is difficult or embarrassing; however, if you truly do love each other, love must also be honest, the more so if there is a significant chance of health risks. What kind of love is it if you hide some (even potential) problem from your partner? What love puts the beloved at risk? And what happens when the problem is discovered? Then it becomes not only a health concern, but a crisis of trust, anger and guilt.

OTHER CONSEQUENCES OF SEX

Perhaps the most obvious possible consequence — and yet frequently forgotten or ignored — is conception: the making of a baby! All too often what should be a wonderful event is turned into a tragedy. The results of that can be truly life-changing, and sadly for the worse. The woman (girl) has to make some very difficult decisions, and life will never be quite the same again. Supportive parents and friends can be a big help, and the modern rush to 'take care of it' through abortion has to be avoided.

The whole subject of abortion is very wide and emotive. However, it is our conviction (both from experience and belief) that abortion simply to destroy an unwanted pregnancy is wrong. Apart from all the ethical

The ultimate object of sexual activity is a baby, who all too often is looked upon as a nuisance instead of being the climax of a relationship.

arguments over the sanctity of life, the woman cannot help but experience loss and guilt — feelings which may last a very long time. Those relatively rare situations of having to choose between the life of the mother or the baby, (life-threatening genetic disorders, rape, incest and so on) are matters of conscience that have to be decided individually. The general situation of abortion because of convenience must be rejected.

Of those who have had abortions of convenience we have counselled, most have expressed their deep feelings of regret. Decisions taken quickly, and sometimes under pressure, are not infrequently seen later as being great mistakes.

Every act of sexual intercourse must be seen as a possibility to conceive, and you must ask yourself, 'Am I ready for motherhood? Can I bring a baby into this situation? Do I have a stable home situation with a loving father?' Parenthood is a tremendous responsibility, and as it says in the marriage vows, not to be entered into lightly.

CONTRACEPTION

Often contraception is suggested as the cure-all for such concerns. The line is: 'If you've taken precautions, then go ahead and enjoy yourself.'

What's wrong with that advice?

▶ Contraception is never 100 per cent foolproof. Contraceptive pills are safe enough — but only if you always remember. And if you're not really intent on a sexual relationship, would you have pills handy if you were carried away by the 'passion of the moment'? Condoms are certainly not totally effective, especially in inexperienced hands. Other methods such as IUDs (intrauterine devices) and diaphragms again are not completely reliable, and require a degree of premeditation (you decide: I'm getting ready for sex).

▶ Condoms provide some protection from the diseases mentioned above, but not total protection. Other forms of contraception do not protect you from infection. Those same risks still apply.

▶ What about those 'mental health' consequences? How will you feel? What about guilt and the loss of self-esteem? Just because you've taken precautions against conceiving, should you really be sexually active? Is this experience really going to be good for you?

▶ What will this do to your relationship? Sex as we have seen can be very destructive — and all too often is not the cement of a relationship but the dynamite that blows it apart. Secret sex in cheap surroundings — is that what you both really want?

MENTAL CONSEQUENCES

Parallel to the physical consequences of sex are the mental and emotional consequences — and they may be even more significant sometimes. The disharmony of giving yourself fully when you cannot honestly make such a commitment, the living of a lie as to what is really happening in your life, the sense of shame or remorse or low self-esteem can lead to further problems.

The problem of guilt is perhaps the most terrible of consequences. Some modern therapists have tried to deal with guilt by denying it. 'You have no need to feel guilty, it's OK,' or so they say. Trouble is, this way of thinking often leads to further problems. For if you can deny your guilt you may end up thinking nothing is wrong, or alternatively your denial of guilt will compound the sense of wrong and make it worse.

Whatever the case, guilt cannot be dealt with by saying it's not there. Guilt craves healing and forgiveness, and to tell someone who believes they are wrong that they are not is surely an even greater wrong!

Damage to your mental health through wrong, perverted or misguided sex is very real. Sleeplessness, anxiety attacks, a feeling of being run-down, trouble concentrating, forgetfulness, headaches — all may have their origins in concerns over

Allowing your life to be obsessed with boys and sexual activity may mean you find difficulty in concentrating on matters which are crucial to your future.

sex. Because sex by definition is supposed to involve another, relationships are very much affected. In sexual wrong there is no 'victimless crime'. For not only are you a victim of your own mistakes, but others are too — innocent or not.

One teenage girl came to us and eventually admitted to a long-standing sexual relationship with a married man. They both realized their affair was wrong, and had often tried to end it. But the physical desire had always proved too strong, whatever their mental decisions. Now they had both become very depressed, and had low self-esteem, particularly due to their inability to end the relationship.

'Confessing' the problem (admitting to a third party) was the first step in preventing and healing the relationship. No longer was it 'their little secret'. Step by step the separation was achieved, gradually making them less dependent upon each other, forcing them to turn their interests elsewhere. And after many months it was safe to say the affair was over, and the rebuilding of their separate selves was beginning. The emotional scars of any such relationship take a long while healing — and yet in order to have some self-respect, this was an essential process.

Wrong sex has its physical dangers which can be identified and measured. But the damage to human lives, feelings and personalities is incalculable, and affects the whole stability of human life, meaning and purpose.

PREVENTION

Prevention is so much better than cure. To make your own decisions rather than allow others to make them for you will increase your self-respect and self-confidence. Just because others are foolish, you don't have to go along with the crowd. The information in this chapter is designed to help you choose, giving you evidence on which to base your choice.

OK, sometimes it's not easy to make logical decisions in the middle of a passionate kiss! So make your decisions beforehand, and stick to them — in that way you'll stay right and also keep your self-esteem.

As a Christian you can be left out of the crowd because you've chosen to be different. It can be harmful but sticking to your own decisions increases your self-respect and confidence.

CONCLUSION

What all this shows is that sex is too powerful and too dangerous to be let loose in a 'free-for-all'. Sex needs to be channelled with love, in a relationship of trust and knowledge. When you are sure that you can relax in the arms of your husband, having confidence that no cross-infecting will occur, maybe practising contraception but not too worried if you do conceive, mentally confident and without guilt or shame — then sex can be brilliant. Otherwise, it will always be less than perfect — damaged goods that will leave you disappointed instead of truly satisfied.

Sex in a relationship of trust and respect is the icing on the cake. When it's just the icing it soon becomes sickly and ordinary.

QUESTIONS AND ANSWERS

Should blood tests be done before marriage — to test for diseases and hereditary problems?

In the US blood tests are routinely carried out before marriage. In most countries this is not done. We imagine that you are asking more specifically about AIDS, as well as other genetic diseases. On the latter, it is important to know of potential problems, although this need not necessarily be a bar to marriage. However, you might then want to consider other options rather than having children, especially if there is a high risk factor. As for AIDS, you would obviously want to know whether this was a real consideration. If your partner has had previous sexual experiences, and may himself be concerned, it might be advisable to be screened for HIV. In most cases it should be clear whether such a blood test is indicated or not. Again absolute honesty is needed in your discussions about sex and previous experiences. Much better that you know the truth from the first rather than feel you have been betrayed later, although it is also important not to become over-anxious if the risk factor is obviously minimal. Counselling might be helpful here.

If your partner has had numerous sexual partners without using sheaths, after marriage would it be all right to *demand* or ask him to use one? I understand HIV has, or can have, a long incubation period.

If you are that concerned and believe there is a genuine risk factor, then a blood test for HIV should give you some reassurance, provided this is done some months after his last sexual partner. We don't know whether 'demanding' is helpful, for as in all sexual matters within marriage this should be by mutual agreement. However, if he is truly kind and loving, and concerned for your welfare, then your husband would surely want to protect you even if the risk was small. Eventually you will need to resolve this as it may become an issue of disagreement at the heart of your most intimate moments and a reminder of a past that may now be regretted. Make sure that you don't use this as a weapon to punish him for previous misdeeds, but treat it purely as a matter of safety.

How can I forgive my partner for his unfaithfulness?

Not knowing your situation it's hard to reply adequately. Forgiveness is something you will have to work at; it doesn't come naturally. Assuming you still hold onto your Christian faith (and sometimes that is damaged by infidelity too) then you will need to pray much, and ask for love and understanding. You will also need to spend time with your partner, once the initial shock has passed somewhat. You will be asking, 'Why?' and feeling hurt and rejected. You will have to be sure that his unfaithfulness is over, and that he is genuinely repentant. You will have to decide whether you want to save your relationship, for the answer is very much in your hands. Accept no excuses (there are none), but try to understand his actions from his perspective. It will feel like rebuilding from ground zero, but if you are willing to try, often the result is a very strong and solid bond, because it has been forged through pain and hardship.

I have so much guilt and shame for something (sexual) I did years ago. Somehow I just can't get away from the negative feelings. What can I do?

This question highlights the damage that sexual mistakes can cause. You don't say exactly what this was and we all respond differently. Certain things appear worse to some, and not so bad to others. Yet we know that you have to deal with this 'worm in the bud' or it will continue to affect your relationships. Just how will depend on your circumstances, and how much others know. We don't believe in laying your burden of guilt on others just to make yourself feel better. Like David in his prayer (read Psalm 51) your primary offence is towards God, and that's the route to take in finding forgiveness and acceptance. Sometimes a non-involved Christian counsellor may be of help, but this may not necessarily be practical or even prudent. If you have wronged someone, you need to try and resolve that — and then, knowing God has forgiven you, forgive yourself. Living in the past prevents you receiving God's blessings in the present, and clouds your current relationship. So once you have finally dealt with the issue, stop looking back and look forward to God's future for you.

Is abortion after rape OK?

In all these ethical questions, to say something is or is not OK is not the right answer. Rape is a terrible crime against an individual's humanity, a destructive evil that takes God's greatest gift of self-giving and turns it into gross selfishness and violent exploitation and abuse. A child conceived through rape, it is argued, will always remind the mother of that rape. On the other hand, should the child pay the ultimate penalty for the sin of his or her father?

In such situations we have to look at the competing claims of those involved — the mother and the baby — and the need to be truly *human*. And that's a choice we hope you never have to face.

Should a Christian doctor prescribe contraceptives if a young unmarried person (Christian) approaches them? (The youth may be, say, 14-16 years old.)

What is worse — illegal sexual intercourse, or the bringing of an unwanted child into this world? Neither are particularly 'good' activities, are they? Our first question is why a Christian girl (presuming female here) of 14 should want contraceptives, and obviously the first approach would be some counselling to discover the situation, since she needs to be warned of the potential problems (other than pregnancy) which such early sex can cause (like cervical cancer). But then, if the young girl is going against all the best advice, and refuses to take any counsel, would you then say, 'I abandon you', and refuse to aid her desire to at least prevent an unwanted child? If the doctor did prescribe contraceptives in such a situation, he or she would not be making the choice for the patient — the choice of whether to be sexually active remains with her.

What have you got to say on contraception? Which is wrong? Which is right?

Again, to say something is wrong or right here is not the issue — unless you call abortion a means of contraception (which it is not, since it is not contraception, for abortion occurs *after* conception has occurred). We do not see any support in Scripture for identifying the normal methods of contraception as sinful. The story of Onan spilling his seed is clearly about breaking God's command to provide for your family.

Other considerations, however, are important in contraception. The Pill is perhaps the most reliable. However, this has shown to have side-effects, especially when taken over long periods. Newer formulations are less harmful. Check with your doctor if you are concerned. The condom (or sheath) is not reliable, but more readily available and has the advantage of providing some protection against sexually-transmitted diseases. IUDs (intrauterine devices, or 'the coil') are less common due to problems of bleeding, and pregnancies in which the device has been incorporated into the growing foetus. The diaphragm (or 'Dutch cap') is used in conjunction with spermicidal (sperm-killing) jelly, but is not entirely effective. Other methods are the 'female condom' (like the condom, but placed in the vagina before intercourse), various spermicidal jellies, creams and sponges, and vasectomy (a surgical procedure that cuts the tubes either from the ovary (female) or the testicles (male). This is meant to be permanent, and is only normally carried out on those who already have the children they desire).

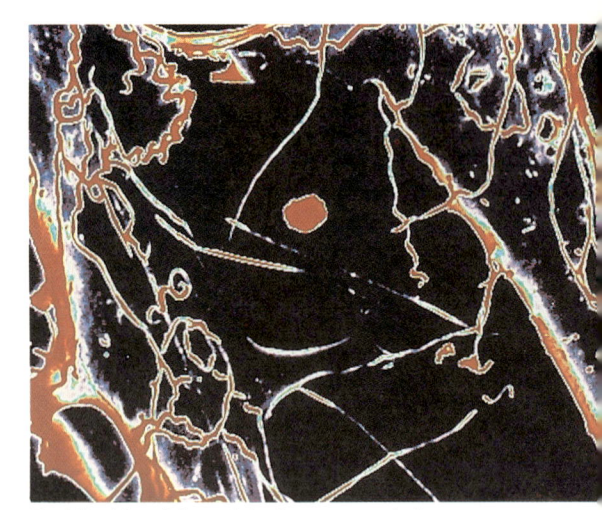

Syphilis (above) is an infectious venereal disease, transmitted through sexual intercourse. If left without treatment it can cause long-term damage to the blood supply, the nervous system, the skin, bones and brain. Gonorrhoea is also spread through intercourse and although not as devastating as syphilis has some nasty effects on the urethra, vagina, cervix and in some cases the uterus and ovaries leading to sterility. It may also affect the rectum, mouth and eyes.

I think I have some kind of infection from having sex. What should I do?

You need to seek medical treatment immediately. Symptoms of sexually-transmitted diseases are often unclear, and you need a doctor to make a diagnosis so that you can receive the correct treatment. If you feel embarrassed about seeing your family doctor, you should go to the local STD clinic (usually at a hospital). Don't try hoping it will go away; that may lead to an infection that can give rise to serious health problems, including infertility. After all that, you will want to rethink your whole life-style, and why you were having sex in the first place.

11

Sexual healing and the God of love

Be merciful to me, O God, because of your constant love. Because of your great mercy wipe away my sins! Wash away all my evil and make me clean from my sin! Psalm 51:1, 2.

SEX AND SALVATION

How is sex involved in salvation anyway? Normally, (at least this is the way most people think) sex only *interferes* with salvation! And yet God's great gift of sexuality, and healing from sexual sin, illustrates the kind of person God is and how He saves us.

Maybe the hardest question is, Why does sexual sin happen to the Christian? After all, you *know* what the rules are. You make a conscious choice not to give in to temptation. And yet you still get into situations you thought were impossible, and end up doing things you greatly regret. So how?

First idea: Maybe you are not so insulated from the way society operates as you think. Attitudes and philosophies about sex are so pervasive that you unconsciously accept them without working things through. Though you may have intellectually decided sex before marriage is wrong, perhaps the way you subconsciously think is different. It's not unusual to have such internal conflicts that may not show up until you're in a decisive situation — and then it may be too late.

For example, if you spend your time absorbing current ideas about sex from the media, don't be surprised if that's the way you end up acting. We decided to check out teen magazines and were surprised with the amount and type of direct and indirect advice these magazines give. A few sample headlines from front covers that we've found:

Sex and my secret lover
Snog-proof makeup
Holidays are for sun, sand and SEX
I had my father-in-law's baby

Boys talk about oral sex
Instant boy-friends
'He got off with six girls in one night'
'My dad dresses up as a woman'
Diary of a 15-year-old mum
SEX RATED! How do you score as a lover?
Sexy Barbie-style fashion

There was not one magazine that didn't have some obviously sexual subject on its cover. Publishers have found that sex sells magazines. And on the inside, the stories, advice, problem pages and the rest churn out a diet of 'if it feels right, do it' philosophy with no moral dimension at all. The reasons to say, 'No': so you're not abused, if it's too soon, if you think you're being pressured. Nothing from a spiritual dimension, of course. And one female TV star reacted to the question of pre-marital sex by saying it was a good idea, and that not having sex before marriage was probably the reason why marriages go wrong!

No wonder girls find themselves adrift in a hostile ocean where, if you don't, you're condemned. So many do, and then regret. And this affects Christians too. But this is hardly love.

Then there's the attitude of individuality, of self-expression. Often twisted and misconstrued and called 'freedom', this modern vice is dangerous when it's applied to areas we know to be wrong. But the idea is firmly rooted in our minds: 'I make the decisions for myself. And no-

From cars to photocopiers, bicycles to bread, sex sends the popular invitation — buy me!

body's going to tell me what to do.' And, we might subconsciously add: 'Not even God.' This preoccupation with self and 'self-fulfilment' is a subtle and demonic trap to fool us into believing that we can choose to go against what we know is right without having to face the consequences. But God doesn't step in to execute punishment; rather He weeps over the results that inevitably come.

Finally, Christians can also become 'mindless' when it comes to the physical moment of sex. So many girls have said, 'I didn't know what I was doing'; 'My mind just seemed to switch off'; 'I just became passive and let him do whatever he wanted'. This robot-like state may be the result of extreme emotion brought on by heavy petting, or maybe the mind's choice to become absent when the going gets tough. Whatever, making no choice is still a choice — and you should have already avoided the potential situation.

GETTING BURNED

We all have to recognize our feebleness. Don't make problems for yourself, and don't move towards the fire just to see how close you can get without being burned. 'The heart is deceitful above all things, and desperately wicked, who can know it?' You can rationalize all you want, but don't put yourself in a situation that may become more than you can handle.

Three ideas: the world, the flesh and the devil — and they can all trip us up. So don't deny their power — and stick with God as Best Friend.

And if you should fail, then remember the Lord who heals.

THE NEED FOR HEALING

Somewhere deep in our innermost selves is the consciousness of how damaged we are, and how much we need to be healed, restored, forgiven. More often than not, this sense of need involves our sexuality, and the way we have expressed it in the past. Skeletons in the cupboard that need removal, hidden agendas that need tearing up, deceptive demons that need to be driven out.

God understands that need. More than that, He understands us — reads us like a book, even those parts we would far rather be secret from everyone. Knowing that He knows is the first step. What a relief — we can finally admit what we may have denied.

The whole purpose for God's coming to humanity was not to condemn, but to save and heal.

God's revelation of salvation through Jesus is expressed in terms

> **LOVE**
> A find, a fire, a heaven, a hell, where pleasure, pain, and sad repentance dwell.
> RICHARD BARNFIELD

of divine healing of the sin-damaged individual. It surely is no coincidence that, having been announced as the one who makes God known (John 1:18), Jesus spent the vast majority of His ministry in acts of physical healing. Jesus told those around Him: '"When he (anyone!) looks at me, he sees the one who sent me"' (John 12:45, NIV), and, '"If you really knew me, you would know my Father as well. From now on, you do know him and have seen him. . . . Anyone who has seen me has seen the Father."' (John 14:7, 9, NIV.)

Christ's main method of demonstrating God to the world was through acts of healing. 'Everywhere he went — into villages, towns or countryside — they placed the sick in the market places. They begged him to let them touch even the edge of his cloak, and all who touched him were healed.' (Mark 6:56, NIV.) A wonderful description of the healing emphasis in the life of Christ.

THE MEANING OF DIVINE HEALING

But that word 'healed' in this text hides a greater truth. The word in the original is the exact same word as used to describe salvation!

As just one example read Luke 7:50 and then compare it with Luke 8:48: '"Your faith has saved you."' '"Your faith has healed you."' (NIV.) Interesting. It's even more interesting when you realize that the actual words in the original are exactly the same. What Jesus told the woman who anointed His feet was the same as what he said to the Syrophoenician woman. The word translated healed in one case and saved in the other is identical.

And then you realize too that the physical healing of the woman's disease (the issue of blood) is equivalent to the salvation healing that Jesus extended to the woman who, in Simon's eyes, was the worst of sinners — a prostitute. Sexual sin is being healed here, and this healing is linked with the statement, '"Your faith has saved you."' Or to interpret: your decision to trust me will allow me to heal the damage done by sin, and save you in my eternal kingdom.

Salvation means healing. Not so much about wiping recorded sins off the slate so that you can start with a clean slate, but healing the disease — the disease of sin. This is so important to realize. God is not checking off sins, seeing whether they are forgiven or not. He's trying to be like a kind and loving doctor, trying to heal us from a corrupting, fatal disease.

That is what Jesus Christ came to do. To win our trust so that because of His gracious nature He could then heal (save) us. This nature and desire is illustrated by those miracles of healing, restoration and cure — revealing God as the one who wants to heal us, not just physically, but spiritually.

Understanding this provides an-

Forgiveness is a sharing, healing experience where the pain of guilt is replaced with a sense of assurance and self-worth.

other insight into one of Jesus' miracles that produced such opposition. In Luke 5 (and the parallels in Matthew 9 and Mark 2) a paralytic man is lowered through the roof into Jesus' presence. Jesus does not say: 'Be healed', or 'Get up and walk.' Instead He points out the healing significance of salvation by saying, '"Friend, your sins are forgiven."' (Luke 5:20, NIV.) Salvation is the healing of the sin damage.

Jesus often spoke to the religious leaders about their problem. He called them 'whited sepulchres' (Matthew 23:27, KJV) because they carefully followed the salvation rules on the outside, but inside were full of corruption. What Jesus wanted to do was to salvation-heal them from the inside, so that then they would be genuinely right on the outside. He told them they were blind. And because they thought they could see, their sin remained. (see Matthew 23:16ff; John 9:41.) Why? Because their arrogant claims to 20-20 vision meant they would not come to Him for salvation-healing. That's why Jesus pronounced so many woes on the scribes and Pharisees — for they, the religious leaders, had failed to understand the truth about God's offer of healing, a spiritual healing that would transform them from being sin-sick rebels to healthy trustworthy friends of God.

THE LORD WHO HEALS

As God said to His people of old, '"I am the Lord who heals you."' (Exodus 15:26, NIV.) This is His salvation — healing all the wounds of sin, curing the sickness of evil, and restoring us once more into full spiritual health: remade into His glorious image. This is His salvation, so fully and freely demonstrated in Jesus and made available to all who want it. This is His salvation: brought to us by God Himself, as He hung there on the cross. Salvation really is healing.

Salvation. We have an old English word that is rather similar. Salve. As Jesus says in Revelation, we're meant to put on eye salve. What for? To cure our spiritual blindness, so that we may see. To heal our eyes. It's the same with sin — even the terrible, unspoken sexual sin. Jesus is not after outward conformity. He wants a cured heart, an attitude that doesn't even want to do wrong, because it is self-destructive. Sexual sin is an obvious example of this — so damaging to self and the heart of relationships.

Jesus announces His ministry by quoting from Isaiah — showing that the God of the Old Testament is just as keen on healing: 'The Sovereign Lord has filled me with his Spirit. He has chosen me and sent me to bring good news to the poor, to heal the broken-hearted . . . .' (Isaiah 61:1, 2. See Luke 4:18.) What a promise! What a clear demonstration of what He wanted to do for the downtrodden, sick and spiritually diseased people around Him.

And what a promise for you too!

IF YOU'VE BEEN HURT

(All these comments are general because we do not know your situation. But they can apply to all kinds of hurts and wrongs that you may have experienced.)

DON'T IGNORE IT

You need to deal with the situation. To let it fester inside you can be the worst thing to do. And if you have been raped, abused or infected that means not just asking God to forgive the one who did this, but going and doing something about it. For it may not only be you, but others — in the past, and in the future too — unless you stop him.

SPEAK TO SOMEONE YOU TRUST

Talk to God, of course, asking for His help in working through all the negative emotions. But talk to trustworthy Christians too. The Bible demonstrates the way in which other believers were able to help those in trouble. This is the way God works — through His followers and the gifts that God gives to each.

LOOK TO GOD FOR HEALING

Healing from pain, anger and bitterness. For if you hold on to these feelings then you will never move past the present. Don't allow whatever wrong was done to you to do more damage through resentment and hatred.

MOVE FORWARD

We are people of hope, and that hope is the renewing process that God does in the present. We leave the past behind us, and press forward towards the mark — the calling of God to an eternal future with Him.

Jesus doesn't just want to clear your bank account of the sin overdraft. He wants to free you from sin sickness. God has always been like that. He has always been 'the Lord who heals you'.

He promises in Jeremiah 3:22 and Hosea 14:4, KJV: 'I will heal their backslidings.' He says in Psalm 147:3, KJV, that 'He healeth the broken in heart'.

'For the Sun of righteousness shall arise with healing in his wings.' See Malachi 4:2.

In response, David cried out to God in Psalm 41:4: '"I have sinned against you, Lord; be merciful to me and heal me."'

SIN-SICK

No question about it. Sin is a terrible sickness of the soul, and God is the only one who can heal us. Suppose you're sick. Maybe you don't even know you're ill. There are many dread diseases in our world today, despite medical advances. Your doctor diagnoses some major problem. Do you ignore it and hope it goes away? Do you pretend nothing's wrong? Or do you go to the only one who can treat you and make you well again? Obvious, isn't it? Even children can see that. When it comes to our spiritual sickness we should listen to the children. They

know more than we do, for we so often turn away from the God who promises to heal us.

Now you've made your choice and have chosen God's way, it's worth sharing your experience and your forgiveness for the attitude of those who found your decision strange.

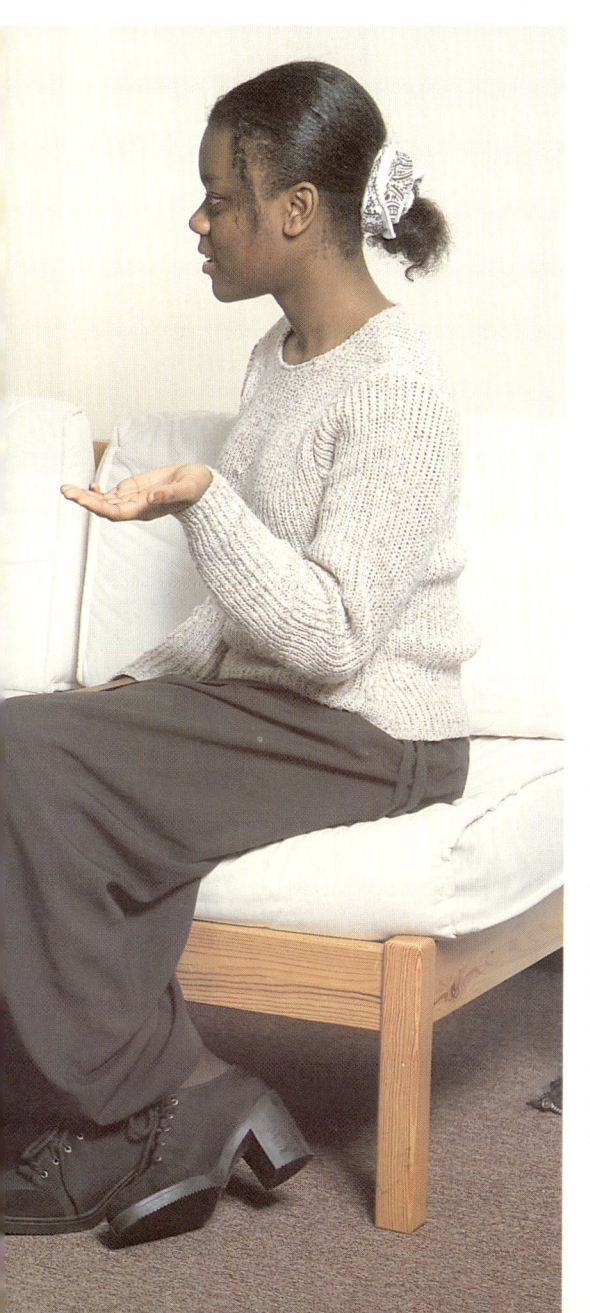

Whose fault is it if we refuse to admit anything is wrong? Or if we tear up the prescription? Or if we secretly flush the pills away? Or if we refuse permission for a life-saving operation?

The very essence of God's good news is healing restoration, but we have to accept that healing, and follow the divine prescription. So how does it work, exactly?

It's summed up in 1 John 1:9. If you have a specific sin, perhaps a sexual sin, then concentrate on these words:

'If we confess our sins, he is faithful and just and will forgive us our sins, and to cleanse us from all unrighteousness.' (KJV.)

Note the progression. First comes confession. You have to admit something's wrong. The healing process cannot occur unless there's recognition of a problem. Added to that must be a desire for change, to be healed from the disease. And this has to be directed to God, asking Him for the help that only He can give. He is faithful and just — He is trustworthy and righteous — and as a result will forgive us our sins. How wonderful the assurance that God can and will forgive all who trust in Him! Even the worst sin, the innermost cancer of sexual sin — however perverted — God can and will forgive. And He doesn't leave it there. With our understanding co-operation He cleanses us from all unrighteousness. He deals with the underlying causes, He repairs and

> If you've been hurt speak to someone you can trust and who you know will listen, won't condemn and will give you the support and confidence to help you leave the past behind.

heals and restores. Forgiveness is not enough. We need complete transformation from selfish rebels sunk in our sexual sin to trustworthy friends who use our sexuality to praise God our Maker and Re-maker.

MADE WHOLE

Only by the power of God can we be made whole again; become *wholesome* instead of selfishly perverse. Responding to God's appeal, 'Come unto me', we receive the divine prescription for the healing of all our sicknesses — especially the mental and spiritual sicknesses that have come from the emotional traumas of wrong sex. The 'soul-sickness' that comes from abusing our sexual gifts can be cured, and we can lift up our faces without shame into the eyes of our loving Saviour.

God heals the mind with its defective thoughts and passions. God heals the damaged emotions that disrupt our lives and destroy our self-worth. God heals the terrible memories, transforming them into examples of His grace. And as with our consent and co-operation God heals, we find grace to forgive and heal those around us who have wronged us. 'Forgive us our trespasses *as we forgive* them that trespass against us.'

SARAH

Sarah had been abused in childhood, and then experienced a whole series of bad relationships; almost as if she was punishing herself for what had happened to her in the past. Her self-perception was near zero; she allowed herself to be humiliated and mistreated by every boy-friend. And only when her life was threatened by all the abuse did she come to her senses and seek help.

Slowly, very slowly, she came to understand what she was doing to herself, and to recognize that without spiritual healing she was lost. Through her deepening relationship with God, and some mature Christian counselling, she finally admitted the mistake of taking responsibility for what she could not have controlled — her childhood abuse. From there, her sexual brokenness was slowly mended, and she no longer craved punishment and mistreatment from the men she chose. After a long time, she began a tentative return to looking for the right relationships, and eventually found a loving, caring man to share her life.

Sarah came back from the spiritually dead. Through spiritual healing she discovered her true self, and the real meaning of love in a God-inspired relationship.

There is nothing that God cannot mend, if we let Him. Abuse, homosexuality, obsession, wrong sex of every kind — all has its cure in the hands of our loving Father. But only, only if we so choose. And God's healing salvation is the proof:

'Let us not love with words or tongue but with actions and in truth. This then is how we know

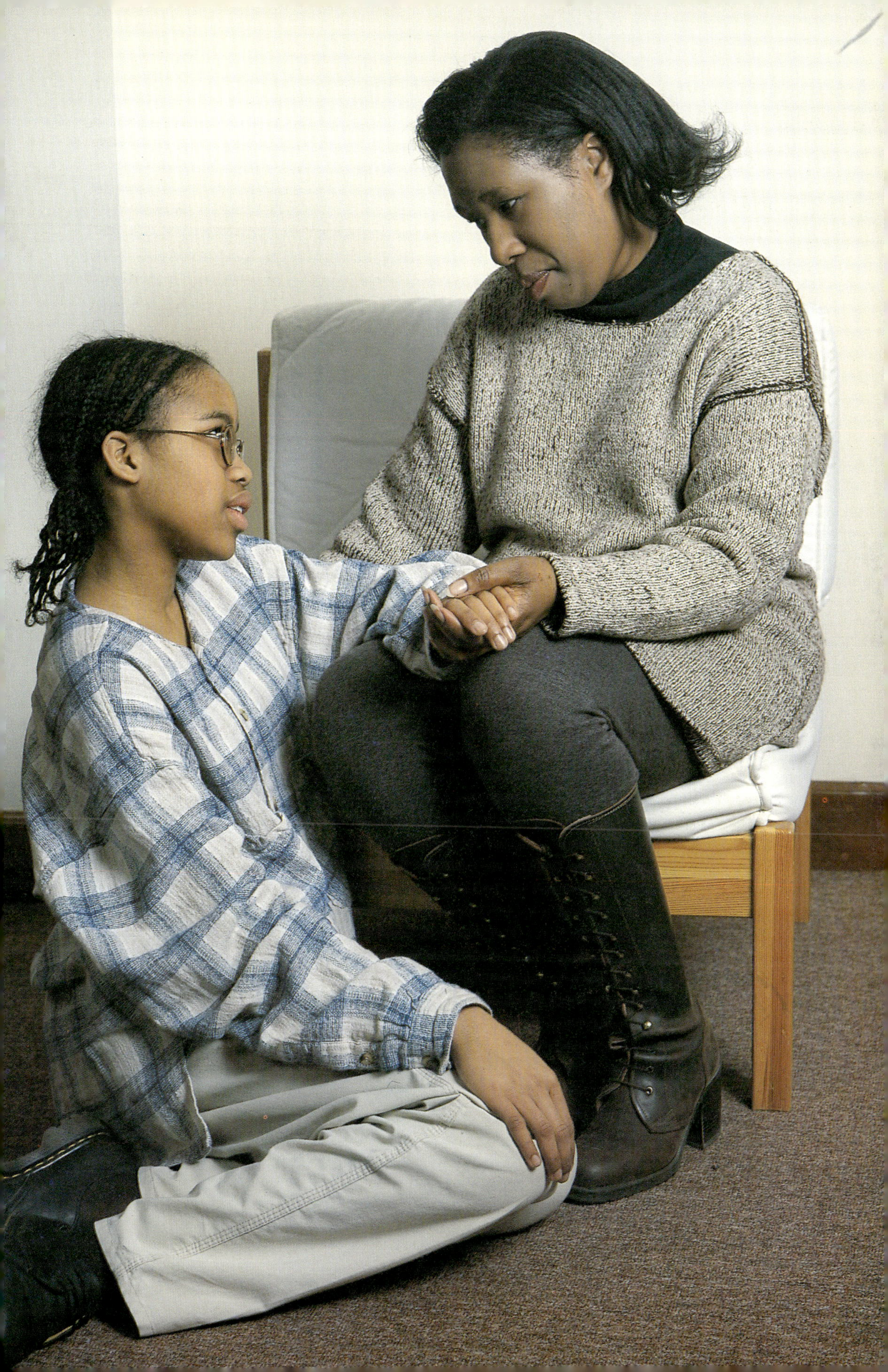

that we belong to the truth, and how we set our hearts at rest in his presence whenever our hearts condemn us. For God is greater than our hearts, and he knows everything.' 1 John 3:18-20, NIV.

THE HEALING PROCESS

Our young daughter came in for some first aid after grazing her knee pretty badly. After the tears, and the cleaning of the wounds, the application of ointment and a lint dressing, she felt better. And yet . . .

'It still hurts.'

'I know. But the worst is over. It'll get better soon.'

'But when? I want it to be all well, right now!'

And we smile. Yet we think we can have that kind of instant healing ourselves, when it comes to healing from the wounds of sexual sin.

It's not that we haven't been forgiven. It's not that God is reluctant to heal, or that He wants us to suffer more! The truth is that the healing process takes time. Our thoughts and desires need the gradual process of re-learning, and the injuries we have done to others and ourselves will require treatment over time, sometimes lengthy treatment over a long time. The process of transformation does not come overnight — we need to grow in understanding too.

Often it's not just a question of a single problem, but many. A whole spider's web of self-deceit and wrong thinking; a whole tubful of past actions and present desires. Just as winning the first battle doesn't win you the war, your choice to be healed from your sexual wrongs doesn't mean instant victory.

But that's no reason not to begin the process. And you need to begin now, wherever you are in your experience. For 'we all have sinned and come short of the glory of God' — and none of us can claim to be righteous. Just remember that Jesus made special time for those who wanted healing from sin, and in particular those who were victims of sexual sin — like Mary Magdalene (a prostitute) and the woman taken in adultery. Pray for the healing only God can give, choose to live differently and think differently, read what God has to say to you in the Bible, and associate with those who will help you in this healing process, not those who will hinder.

SUGGESTED PRAYER

Lord, I know what kind of person I really am. I couldn't hide that from you, even if I wanted to. And I'm glad you see me as I really am too, because then I don't have to explain it all. I recognize my sins, especially today my sins in the area of sex.

I agree that I have done what is wrong, and I am not excusing myself. I take responsibility for my own actions. And I ask you to forgive me.

More than that, I want to be made new again, as you promise. I want to live without sexual sin, I want to be able to say 'No' to temptation, and to be happy with the way I express the sexuality you gave me. Please heal me from the damage of my sexual sins, help me to forgive those who have wronged me, and give me the strength to live as you would want.

Trusting in you, God my friend . . .

THE UNFORGIVABLE SIN?

One last thought here. Sexual sin is not the unforgivable sin. Because it seems so major to us does not mean that we should specifically single out sexual sin as being the worst or the unforgivable sin. The Church has not always handled sexual sin well, and by its actions has perhaps suggested that this is one area where forgiveness and acceptance is hard to achieve. Because attitudes to sex have been problematic within the Church (look again at the chapter on God and Sex) there is no reason to come down harder on sexual sin than on other aspects of evil. That's not to say sexual sin is in any way acceptable, or that it should not be condemned, or that it is not particularly damaging especially in human relationships.

Sexual sin makes us all uncomfortable, and we comprise the church. But we must try to deal with sexual sinners redemptively, and show them the way back, to reveal in our own lives God's graciousness, and to make sure we never reject any one of God's fallen children.

Don't be put off by those who consider God to be a rather fierce and unbending character. He wants you to talk to Him as you would an understanding and forgiving friend.

QUESTIONS AND ANSWERS

I know God has forgiven me for having sex without being married. But how do I forgive myself?

One of the hardest questions — because we may almost *want* to suffer as a way of feeling we're being punished for doing wrong. Also involved is the whole concept of self-perception — how do I see myself? What do you tell yourself: 'I'm a bad girl and I've done all these wrong things . . . ', and then go on to remind yourself of everything evil and sinful? Unless you can catch a glimpse of being someone better, of understanding that God sees great potential in you, it *will* be hard to forgive yourself. But until you do, you can't move forward. And to say that you can't forgive yourself, even though God can, is being rather arrogant, isn't it? We need to be careful that we don't throw God's healing forgiveness back in His face. See yourself for what you are, certainly, but then see what you (with God) can be. And don't wallow in your own self-rejection!

How can I show others that I've really changed? In particular my boy-friend who still wants to go on doing what we did before?

How do you convince someone about any change in attitude and behaviour? In that sense sexual attitudes and behaviour are no different — you have to communicate exactly what you think and what you want to happen. The trouble with sex is that it is often surrounded by confused and confusing signals — saying no when you mean yes and all that. So in speaking and behaving with your boy-friend, you have to be crystal clear. No does absolutely mean no, and not 'I'm playing hard to get'. And back up what you *say* with what you *do* — don't let your actions give a lie to your words.

I feel I keep on letting God down every time I get involved with a boy. Is this wrong?

Depends on what you're thinking and what you're doing. If by being 'involved' you mean sexual intercourse or a similar substitute, then the guilt feelings are trying to get you back on the right track. If you're just worried that God's going to be jealous or something if you fall in love with a boy, then of course not! But do remember that your relationship with God and salvation are more important than anything else — or anyone else.

I love my boy-friend but we don't seem to get on, especially physically. Sometimes I feel that even when things are good they're bad, and I get really depressed. And God seems a long way away.

Not even a question, just a statement. It's hard even to begin to answer since you don't give much information. Certainly you express a tension between your spiritual life and your boy-friend relationship. Maybe you don't share the same goals, maybe you're not planning to stay together anyway. Perhaps you've had a heavy sexual relationship that no longer seems right; or is it that what you thought would be wonderful no longer satisfies? Like a sign on the side of a church, 'If God seems a long way away, who moved?' It wasn't God, and if your current relationship and way of life have taken you away from God then it cannot be good for you. Take time to rediscover God, experience His healing forgiveness, and decide what you really want in life!

Take time to rediscover God, search out His promises in the Bible, learn to pray again, have time to think. Thank God for His generous care and love for you.

12

The promise

I am my lover's and my lover is mine. Song of Songs 6:3, NIV.

PROMISES, PROMISES...

Sex has been so distorted and perverted that you can easily become negative and defensive. The purpose of this chapter is to make sure sex is seen as good and positive — not as a problem to be dealt with. You can review the previous chapters if you have particular problems. Here we shall celebrate God's glorious creation of our sexuality. We want to understand the meaning of the promise: God's promise to us, our promise to God, and our promise to each other and to ourselves.

What's so good about sex? How does being sexual make me a better person? Why did God make us sexual if He knew there were going to be so many problems?

WHY SEX?

Why sex? Because this is the way God designed us, to make us look out from ourselves and actually want to be part of someone else.

The concepts of togetherness, partnership, and intimacy reflect what God wants for us. Being made in the image of God has more to do with the way we think than the way we look. So there's a sense in that sex is reflecting God: especially the intimate relationship He wants with every intelligent being in His creation.

> **SEX**
> **The sign that the lovers have nothing to refuse each other; that they belong wholly to each other.**
> JACQUES LECLERCQ

And so God was willing to run all the risks that come with making sexual beings, particularly after the Fall. Our sexuality is important beyond creating children and experiencing pleasure. It is being like God in His union and communion. In Ephesians that's made clear. And so when we make love we are thinking God's ways after Him, we are mirroring His self-giving creative love for those who will respond to Him.

Sometimes Christians are worried by the statement of Jesus that there will not be marrying or giving in marriage after the resurrection. But bear in mind that Jesus was primarily answering a question about the validity of the resurrection, not about relationships in heaven, and also that the term 'marrying and giving in marriage' is also used to describe a world that is unconcerned about God (see Matthew 24:38, KJV). Jesus is not defining what kind of relationship will exist in the kingdom between people who are married now — and it would be inconceivable that the one person you have such an intimate relationship with here will not be equally (if not more) special in the hereafter. Jesus also reminded those who have doubts as to what the future holds that 'Eye hath not seen . . . .' (1 Corinthians 2:9, KJV.) Remember that it was God who invented sex, that this was not specifically designed as a remedy for sin (male and female were created in Paradise!), and that this will be even better in God's future for you and me. That we will be in character like the angels does not mean we shall become sexless, rather it describes the harmonious, pure and selfless relationships of heaven.

Many descriptions of God's future are parallels of the world before sin. Since God made Adam and Eve as sexual beings in the first place, and our characters are moulded by that sexuality, then when Paradise restored is finally achieved, we do not expect to be disappointed!

CELEBRATING GOD

However, we're willing to leave all that in the hands of our loving Father. What is more significant is the way we see things now. Unless

The closeness, the partnership and the intimacy found in a genuine relationship is just what God planned for us. It's a great reminder of the way He feels for us all, good or bad.

we understand the specialness of God's gift of sex then it will always be something less than wonderful, and perhaps even just a mechanical act to be accomplished, a duty to be performed. In so many ways, great sex is not about technique or performance, despite what the sex manuals say. Great sex is the mutually-bonding experience that brings assurance and confidence, that says, 'You are the most special person to me.' Great sex celebrates God as not only the Creator of physical bodies that experience pleasure but the Giver of joy 'inexpressible' to the spiritual mind.

Perhaps that's where Christians still have their reservations. Inhibited by preconceptions about sex, they also suppress their expression of sexuality for fear of displeasing God. Sexual sensations are so overwhelming and scary that to be able to abandon yourself in such a sea of passion means you have to be supremely confident of both God and your partner! You cannot truly experience the totality of sexual abandonment if you're forever thinking 'I must keep at least one foot on the floor' — as the actors and actresses of a previous Hollywood generation actually did in order not to offend the censors!

Such a surrender is not a giving over to lust, but a surrender in love to one in whom you have complete trust. *And that is why casual sexual intercourse can never be right — for in that situation the surrender of self in loving trust can never happen.* As someone once said of his adulterous relationship, 'It was just not enough.' And whatever the feelings, whatever the thoughts of love, it can never be enough — because the completeness of total self-giving and

The traditional Christian view of sexual attraction as being rather distasteful has meant many are inhibited by the fear of upsetting God.

honest trust will always be absent.

Making love within marriage is a form of worship. In the old marriage vows was the line, 'With my body I thee worship.' That's not idolatry, unless you make your partner more important than God. But in 'worshipping' each other through the body — and that includes all aspects of the physical, not just intercourse — we also worship God: Creator, Healer, Restorer, Forgiver, Saviour. That God is so intimately involved disturbs some. They find it disconcerting that God should be there in the bedroom, and feel inhibited as if He were looking over their shoulders.

But God is not like that. He is not glaring at us if we experience pleasure. Neither does He have some prurient interest in our sexual behaviour. In intimate relationships, as in everything else, God simply wants the best for us. For if we experience the best of God's creative abilities we will want to praise the God who made us that way, who encourages our full personal development, and who is delighted with the worship we bring to Him through our own sexual celebrations.

Counselling a Christian couple over this aspect of God's involvement, we found they were both uncomfortable with their sexuality, and saw this as some kind of necessary evil. The husband expressed it as: 'I know sex is OK, but if I think about God I just can't do it.' Only through a biblical study of not only the gift of sex but God's endorsement of sexual pleasure (noting particularly that the Bible includes the Song of Solomon!) were this couple able to bring God into their sexual relationship, with all the joys that brings.

We remember a church minister's wife who had been brought up to see sex as something unpleasant, as nasty and ugly. She was a lovely person, kind and affectionate. But because of these ingrained ideas, their mutual experience was less than the best it could be. A tragedy that could be prevented by the church speaking straight about the true beauty of God's design of human sexuality.

TWO BECOMING ONE

Read again the exquisite description of the first marriage in Eden (Genesis 2:21-25). Take in the depth of meaning of the statement that 'they became one flesh'. Most sex in our world today is a quick physical joining that has as much meaning as eating a sandwich. But in the beginning it was not so — it was the blending, merging and unifying of two into one. One in mind, body and spirit. That's the height of the ultimate relationship between man and woman, and leaving out one aspect diminishes the rest. This is the 'one flesh experience' — more important than achieving orgasm, slaking lust or providing satisfaction. It is this concept of bonding — entering into such a close union that you both submerge yourselves in

A hazard to good relations is the common practice of regularly doing your own thing when your partner would appreciate doing something together occasionally.

something greater. Only something we can grasp at now, but it was fully God's intention and remains so.

When Jesus was asked about marriage (and the questions were never positive — they were asked in the context of divorce, etc), Jesus showed God's plan and promise. The Pharisees tried to test Jesus about legitimate reasons for divorce. Always concerned about their legal standing before God, these Pharisees reflect humankind's preoccupation over rules and regulations instead of right relationships, especially with God.

Jesus emphasizes the basics of relationships in His answer: '"Haven't you read," He replied, "that at the beginning the Creator 'made them male and female', and said, 'For this reason a man will leave his father and mother and be united to his wife, and the two will become one flesh'? So they are no longer two, but one. Therefore what

God has joined together, let man not separate.'" (Matthew 19:4-6, NIV.)

And to be truly joined you need to grow and develop together — it doesn't happen overnight. Here, as in much of life, communication is the key. 'Speak the truth in love' is the command of Paul to his friends in Ephesus. You can speak the truth, and be as hard as stone, as sharp as steel, as bitter as gall. You can speak in love, and lie through your teeth. Make it your motto always to speak the truth in love together. The result: 'Speaking the truth in love, we will in all things grow up into him who is the Head, that is, Christ.' (Ephesians 4:15, NIV.)

Neither is communication always speaking, but mutually understanding — and *wanting* to know the other more and more. No private lives, no separate holidays, no fragmented life-styles — but time and space shared together in the most intimate ways.

LOOKING FORWARD

We don't know where you are. Nervously teetering on the edge of adolescence and adulthood, anxiously wondering. Battered and scarred from bitter experiences of

Sharing quality time doing things you enjoy together is an important part of finding out more about how you both tick.

Choosing a partner who also likes you is sometimes a difficult and frustrating exercise but don't rush in — it's the most important decision in your life.

the past. Wonderfully in love with the guy of your dreams. Wherever. But be sure of one thing as you look forward to the future — don't short-change yourself. Your choice of partner is probably the most important decision you will ever make. We say that advisedly, since even a decision for God and to become a Christian can be greatly affected by who you choose.

We don't want to paint an over-romantic vision of the future, but a realistic expectation of joy and fulfilment, both physically and spiritually. That's why your choice of husband is so important, and if you're only looking at one aspect you'll be disappointed.

If he gives all the impressions of being a great lover — what about his spiritual commitment? And what happens when the passions fade and you find out how incompatible you both are? Great sex cannot make a marriage!

But then again almost any other single reason for marriage can be 'wrong'. Marriage is based on a whole variety of reasons; even to say 'I love him' is not enough. An understanding of temperaments is vital; without communication any relationship is doomed; there must be common ground — general agreement on the basic principles and goals in life. ('Can two walk together, except they be agreed?' asks God in Amos 3:3, KJV.) Most of all, without God, marriage can never reach its maximum potential.

Money ranks high as a cause of marriage breakdown. Learn to manage your finances and share the decisions you make. It will help you avoid confrontation when money is scarce and there are bills to pay.

And maybe the disciples were unconsciously right when they responded to Jesus, '"If this is the situation between a husband and a wife, it is better not to marry."' (Matthew 19:10, NIV.) If there is not that God-filled love, the marriage can be a liability, a curse, a disaster.

And to those who fear loneliness if they do not marry we would say, Remember: you were made individual but not alone.

GOD'S PROMISE

So what is the promise for you?

God's promise relates to what you choose. As in any area of life, what

General agreement on the basic principles of what life is about is essential. Many rely on love and sex to hold a relationship together only to find that they are of little use when problems and disagreements turn the heat up.

God can do for you is limited by the choices you make, and how open you are to His guidance and help. In the same way as a mother may love her wayward son, God still loves us. And yet that mother may not be able to do as the son asks, or may even appear to be unco-operative, realizing that love does not mean assisting in evil or aiding in activities that will eventually damage.

And as we saw in a previous chapter, marriage is not necessarily the great ideal for all — nor is it always possible. For some, marriage becomes the supreme desire, the ultimate objective. But God must be above all this, and singleness with God is far better than marriage without God.

Nor are there any absolute guarantees. God cannot make your chosen boy fall in love with you! He does not interfere with our choices;

He certainly will not meddle with your freedom or that of anyone else. If He wished to do that, God would have controlled things from the beginning — and we would have ended up as robotic agents following God's predetermined course.

So while we pray for happy marriages and a fulfilled loving, sexual experience, much lies in our own hands. We cannot expect God to make right what we choose to do wrong in our marriages — for in these most intimate relationships God is involved but does not dictate. Healing, cure, salvation, restoration — all this and more — but forcing love, obedience, happiness, submission, no. God chose not to do that, and we cannot do this either. Only by love is love awakened, and how you choose to relate is down to you.

That is why the promises made during the wedding service are so important. They are not just words

Being single can be a fulfilled and enjoyable lifestyle, certainly better than being married to someone who doesn't share your principles and ideals.

to be recited. More than a legal contract, more than a pledge of loyalty, marriage vows are a declaration of an inner attitude. You *choose* your partner and *commit* yourself to him in a way totally different to anyone else. Apart from your relationship to God, your relationship to your husband is to be more special than to anyone else.

So to those who say that 'marriage is just a piece of paper' we would respond, 'That's true if you see marriage that way.' If marriage is only some paper contract, then it will be just as easily disposed of as any other such contract. But if it expresses your determined and decided commitment, your freely-given and thought-through *promise*, then marriage means so much more.

Why is a piece of paper so important?

Try that one on the next policeman who asks to see your driving licence! Like any other important document, it speaks about responsibility, taking our actions seriously, about being really committed. Of course, it can't be like a contract: when you want your husband to love you more, you can't pull out your marriage certificate and demand he fulfils its obligations! But it does symbolize what you both have agreed to, and confirms to all your mutual decision to make a life, family and home together.

A God-filled marriage is a symbol of God's oneness with the believer both now and in the eternal future.

> A wedding is a demonstration of the commitment that is an essential part of a successful, long-term partnership. It's a vow that emphasizes a thought-through promise compared with lightly conceived relationships that often fail because of the lack of commitment.

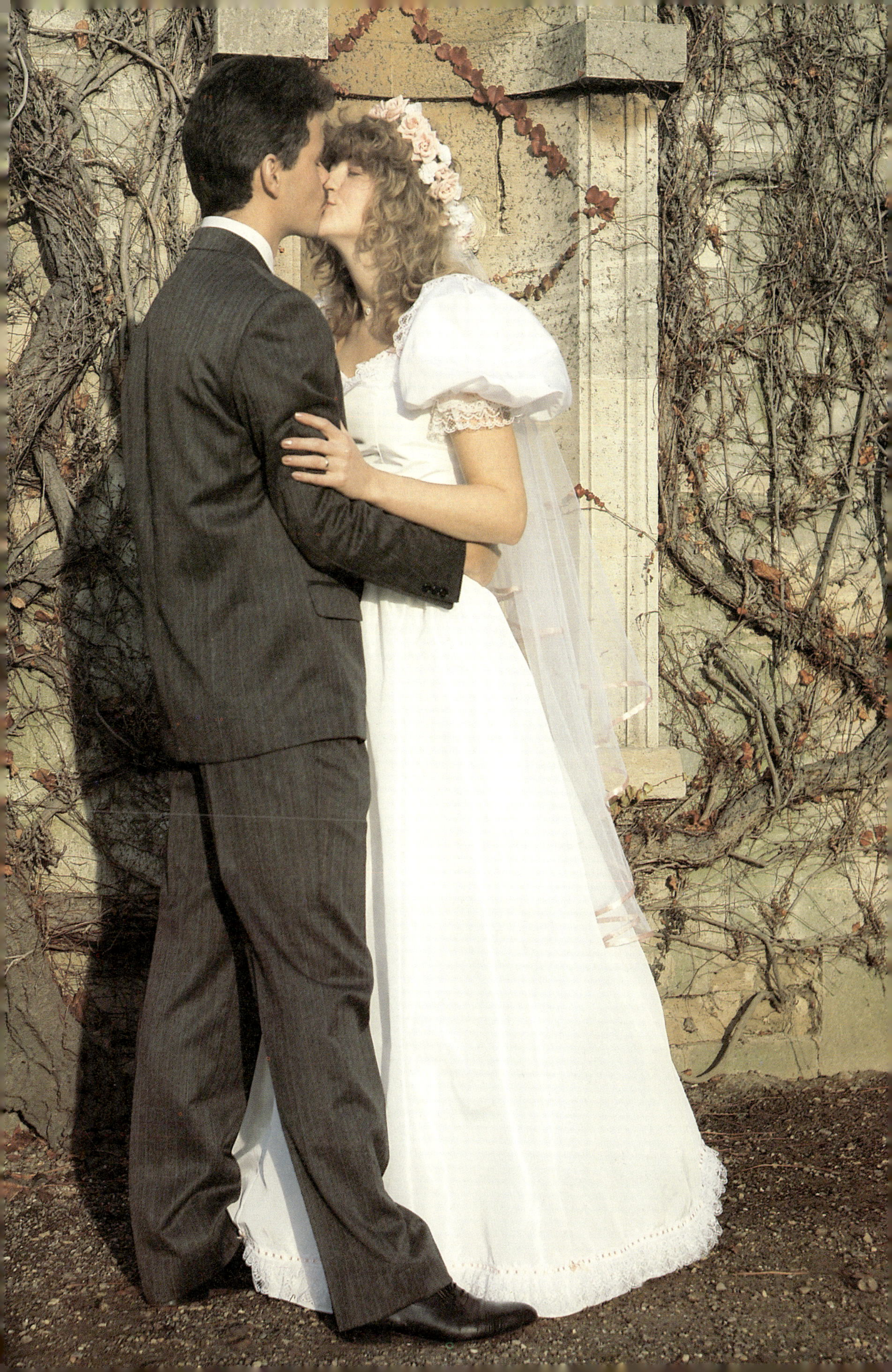

TRUE LOVE IS WILLING TO WAIT

'I've realized that I have a special gift that I can give only once. It's a very intimate part of me — a very private place and a very private part. And I want to make that present the best it can be. I also love myself enough not to want to spoil that gift. I can see that love has deeper meanings — maybe even meanings I can't see now as a teenager. So I don't want to get fooled. And so I tell anybody who asks that I will only give myself in this special way to the one I marry. Because true love is willing to wait. I'm willing to wait. And only the man who is willing to wait is worth my special gift.'

ESTHER

MY PROMISE TO MYSELF

Take the time to write out your promise to yourself about your future sexual behaviour. What are you going to do? What are you not going to do?

And then pray to God for the strength to keep your promise.

Being married to someone who loves you and shares the same Christian principles is an ideal environment in which children can feel wanted, loved and secure. That's a family, a home, that's what God intended marriage to be.

In the imagery of Revelation the woman, the Bride, represents the new Jerusalem (21:2); who gives the invitation: 'The Spirit and the bride say, "Come!" And let him who hears say, "Come." Whoever is thirsty, let him come; and whoever wishes, let him take the free gift of the water of life.' (22:17, NIV.)

We wish for you God's promised happiness for the present, and an eternal life for the future, and the counsel of the Spirit as you make your decisions and develop your relationships of love. Most of all may God guide you in your special relationship of highest love and total commitment.

INDEX

Page numbers in italics indicate diagrams

Abortion 11, 68, 69, 139, 140, 147, 148, 154, 155
Abuse 14, 128, 130, 141, 163, 166
Acceptable behaviour 10
Acceptance 154
Action 27
Adolescence 128, 177
Adultery 10, 14, 27, 64, 94, 101, 106, 126, 127, 137, 138, 140, 141, 168, 174
Adults 110, 177
Affairs 94, 151
Age 108, 109
AIDS 14, 19, 42, 68, 69, 143-147, 153
Alcohol 74, 103, 132
Animalistic sex 72, 135
Anger 27
Anus (herpes) 145
Anxiety attacks 149
Arousal 16

Baby 18, 37-39, 47, 68, 104, 140, 142, 143, 147, 148, 154
Background 109
Balanced characteristics 97
Betrayal 10, 114
Biochemicals 29
Bladder *39*
Blindness 119, 124
Blisters (genital) 143
Blood 37, 143, 144, 160
  transfusion 144
Body cycles 36
  fluids 143, 144
Breast enlargement 76
  implants 76
Breasts 37, 41, 43, 45-48, 51, 76, 110, 118
Broken sex 126, 134, 136-139
Buttocks 110

Cancer 143, 145, 146, 155
Career moves 27, 104, 106
Caressing 29, 40, 101, 110, 118
Caring 97
Casual sex 94, 142
Celibacy 83
Cervical cancer 143, 146, 155
Cervix *39*
Cheap pulp novels 133
Children 109, 127, 128, 144, 172
Chlamydia 143
Climax 101, 116
Clitoris 39, *39*, 41, 43, 47, 116, 118
Coccyx *39*
Coil 156
Cold sores 143
Communication 27, 29, 100, 170, 177, 179
Computer dating 96
Concentration 149
Conception 38, 140, 147-149, 152
Concubines 94, 128
Condoms (sheath) 143, 144, 148, 155
Confession 127
Conscience 101
Consideration 97
Contraceptive pills 98, 148, 154, 155
Contraception 11, 93, 139, 148, 152, 154, 155
Counselling 106
Courtship 95, 109
Cream (spermicidal) 156
Creation 31
Cross-infection 152
Cuddling 41, 109, 139

Date rape 131
Dating 34, 95, 96, 98, 103, 104
Daydreaming 106
Deception 127, 140
Denial 133

Diaphragm (Dutch cap) 148, 156
Diarrhoea 145, 146
Discos 103
Disease 104, 124, 125, 143, 148, 160, 165
Dishonesty 126
Distrust 114
Divine healing 160
Divorce 14, 58, 64, 69, 84, 114, 127, 176
Doubt 114
Dreams 36, 106, 119, 127
Drug addicts 144
Drugs 14, 74, 103, 113, 132, 144, 146, 147
Dutch cap (Diaphragm) 148, 156

Egg (ovum) 37-39, *39*
Ejaculation 47, 124
Embryo (zygote) *39*
Emotional consequences 149
Engagement 114
Enjoyment 14, 27
Epileptic fits 119
Erection 10, 44, 46, 51
Erotic act 119
Excitement 51
Experiences 25
Explicit sex 133
Extramarital sex 94

Fallopian tube (oviduct) *38, 39, 40*
Fantasies 36, 68, 108, 120, 121, 140
Father 130
Female attractiveness 43
    condom 156
    form 133
    identity 133
    sexuality 95
Fertility rituals 79
Fertilization 37, *40*
Fever 143
Fimbria *38*
First approach 98
Flirting 35
Flu 146
Foetus *39*, 140, 156
Foreplay 139
Forgetfulness 149
Forgiveness 103, 125, 127, 138, 149, 153, 154, 166, 169, 170

Fornication 111
Free sex 74
Friendship 35, 95-98, 110
Frigidity 46, 125

Gastrointestinal problems 145
Gay people 136
Genital cancer 143
    blisters 143
    herpes 143
    irritation 143
    warts 68, 143
Genitals 41, 68, 102, 110, 114, 116, 118, 119, 143
Genetic abnormalities 136
    conditions 140
    disease 153
    disorders 148
    make-up 139
Girls 124
Glandular activity 29
Going all the way 123
    out 95
    steady 95
    too far 100, 101
Gonorrhoea 68, 118, 143
Good listening skills 97
Gratification 116
Guilt 10, 42, 68, 108, 111, 112, 114, 125, 141, 148, 149, 152, 154

Hatred 132
Headaches 143, 146, 149
Healing 112, 160, 162, 163, 165, 166, 168, 169, 181
Heavy music 103
Hereditary problems 153
Heredity 34
Herpes simplex 143, 145
Heterosexuality 144
Holding hands 40
Homosexuality 136, 137, 139, 144, 146, 166
Honesty 97
Hormone irregularities 136
Hormones 13, 29, 36, 43, 106
Human immunodeficiency virus (HIV) 143, 144-146, 153
    relationships 58

Humour 97
Husband 11, 35, 40, 58, 70, 104, 108, 127, 128, 141, 144, 152, 182
Hymen *39*, 40
Hypodermic needles 144

Idolatry 137
  of sex 79
Illegitimate pregnancies 11, 64
Illicit sex 118
Immaturity 108
Immorality 64, 137
Immoral thoughts 108
Immune system 144
Improper behaviour 128
Incest 69, 128, 148
Incubation period of HIV 153
Infatuation 133, 142
Infection 104, 142, 143, 145, 156
Infertility 119, 143, 156
Infidelity 10
Inherited guilt 111
Insanity 119
Intimacy 68, 84, 86, 88, 90, 91, 102, 116, 121, 122, 134, 153, 184
Intimate relationships 94
Intercourse 18, 38, 40-42, 46, 47, 51, 55, 63, 79, 82, 84, 88, 92, 101, 111-114, 116, 118, 123, 125, 136, 139, 143, 144, 148, 154, 156, 170, 174, 175
Irritable 36
Intrauterine device (IUD) 148, 156

Kaposi's sarcoma 146
Kissing 29, 40, 41, 51, 54, 80, 88, 90, 92, 101-103, 105, 109, 110, 116, 125, 139, 151

Labia 39, *39*
Language differences 109
Late night sessions 118
Lesbian 125
Libido 34, 46
Listening 25, 97
Living together 94
Loneliness 31, 121
Loss, feelings of 148
Love at first sight 59

Lust 70, 116, 132, 137, 140, 174, 175
Lying 140
Lymph glands 145

Madness 133
Magazines 9, 10, 45, 64, 106, 133, 157, 158
Making love 106
Maladjustment 111
Marital problems 75
Marriage 10, 14, 16, 19, 22, 33, 42, 53, 55-59, 63, 65, 92, 94, 96, 98, 104, 106, 108-114, 119, 121, 123, 125, 126, 127, 130, 140, 142, 148, 153, 157, 158, 170, 173, 175, 176, 179-184
Mastectomy 76
Masturbation 18, 41, 44, 46, 47, 92, 101, 116, 118-121, 124
Maturity 108, 110
Menstruation (periods) 29, 36-39, 68, 98, 118
Mental consequences 149
  dimension 72
Misguided morality 111
Mistreatment of others 126, 130
Mistresses 94
Money worries 27
Monkeys 144
Morality 11, 14, 16, 18, 50, 52, 64, 97
Mosquitos 144
Motherhood 148
Movies 106
Multiple partners 66
Murder 127, 140
Mutual understanding 110
Myths 66

Nakedness 110, 133
Nationality 109
Nightmares 36
Nipples 51, 118
Non-Christian relationships 59

Obsession 132, 133, 166
Oral sex 47, 92, 101, 116, 118, 123, 139, 143
Orgasm 40, 41, 43, 45-47, 116, 123, 175
Ovary 37, *38*, *39*, *39*, *40*, 156
Oviduct (fallopian tube) *38*, *39*, *40*
Ovum (egg) 37-39, *39*

Parenthood 130 148
Parties 74, 132
Partners 128, 140, 144, 147, 153, 179
Passion 71, 108, 174
Pelvis 143
Penetration (intercourse) 101, 102
Penicillin 143
Penis 40, 41, 44, 46, 47, 51, 116, 118, 143
Periods (menstruation) 29, 36-39, 68, 98, 118
Perversions 135, 136
Petting 41, 109, 118, 125, 139, 159
Physical abuse 141
   acts 101
   assault 128
   consequences 149
   desires 34
   dimension 72
   emotion 29
   enjoyment 43
   intimacy 95
   pleasure 79, 122
   processes 29
   relationship 109
   response 34
   stimulation 29
Pill, contraceptive 98, 148, 154, 155
Pleasure 14, 29, 43, 70, 82, 90, 100, 103, 120, 172, 175
Pneumonia 145
Polyandry 94
Polygamy 94
Pornography 68, 108, 133, 134, 140
Post-coital depression 42
Pregnancy 19, 38, 42, 68, 92, 93, 104, 124, 136, 139, 140, 143, 146, 147, 155, 156
Premarital counselling 56
   sex 9, 10, 14, 65, 94, 109, 113, 114, 123, 125, 158
Pre-menstrual tension (PMT) 36
Prevention 151
Procreation 83
Prostitution 79, 133-135, 137, 140, 146, 160, 168
Puberty 13, 29, 34, 37
Pubic hair 37

Race 109
Rape 69, 128, 130-133, 139, 140, 148, 154, 163
Rapid ageing 146
Rectum *39*
Rejection 97, 133
Repentance 127
Repression (sexual) 46
Reproduction 37, 93
Reproductive cycle 36
   organs 38, *38*
Respiratory infection 145
Response 25, 44, 133
Retarded emotional development 136
Romance, spiritual 104, 105
Romantic affair 127
Rules 30

Safe sex 42, 143, 144
Salvation 157, 159, 160, 162, 170, 181
Sanitary pads 38
Second marriages 127
Secrecy 126, 149
Self-assurance 97
   -centredness 126
   -control 110
Selfishness 43, 127, 131
Self-worth 112
Semen 38, 41, 47, 118, 119 124, 143, 144
Sense of humour 97
Sensitivity 97
Sensuality 34
Separation 141
Sex clinics 77
   manuals 27
   shops 133
Sexual abuse 128
   activity 100, 142
   acts 133
   arousal 133
   behaviour 123
   desires 86, 133
   difficulties 75
   drive 43, 46, 124
   frustration 124, 140
   images 106
   objects 134
   organs 37, 101

perversions 14, 80, 135, 136
problems 78
relationships 60
response 44, 133
satisfaction 79
secretions 143
sins 91
thoughts 106, 121
taboos 78
values 78
Sexuality, women's 133
Sexually-transmitted diseases (STD) 11, 69, 118, 142, 143, 147, 156
Shame 114
Sheath (condom) 153, 155
Sickness 166
Single person 95
Skin conditions 145
Sleeping together 69, 78
 with opposite sex 109
Sleeplessness 149
Solo sex 120, 124
Sperm 37-39, *39*, 124, 156
Spermicidal cream 156
 jelly 156
 sponge 156
Spiritual bonding 68
 dimension 72
 healing 162
 union 72
Stimulation 39-41, 43, 44, 47, 50, 101, 116, 118, 120, 139
Stroking 40, 118
Suspicion 114
Syphilis 68, *156*

Tampons 38, 40
Temptation 16, 18, 19, 102, 105, 109, 134, 157
Ten Commandments 126
Tenderness 108
Tension 120
Testicles 156
Thighs 110
Touching 18, 29, 40, 100-102, 110, 118
Trustworthiness 97

Uncertainty 114
Unfaithfulness 153, 154
Urethra 124
Urination 143
Urine 40, 124
Uterus (womb) 37, 38, *38*, 39, *39*, *40*, 41, 43

Vagina 37-39, *39*, 40, 41, 43, 47, 116, 118, 124, 143, 156
Vasectomy 156
Venereal disease 142
Verbal attacks 128
Vibrator 125
Videos 133
Violence 133
Virginity 29, 40, 104, 108, 123, 138, 146, 147
Virus 143-145
Visual images 43, 45, 110
 stimulation 76

Warts (genital) 68, 143
Wedding night 40
Weight loss 145
Wet dreams 119
Wives 11, 70, 94, 127, 128, 144
Womb (uterus) 37, 38, *38*, 39, *39*, *40*, 41, 43
Wrong impressions 98

Zygote (embryo) *39*

PHOTOGRAPHERS

ACE PHOTO AGENCY
Mauritius 17, 152, 176, Ian Spratt 41, 128, 129, Bill Backmann 103, David Kilpatrick 130, Phototake 146, Michael Bluestone 148, 155, 185.

AUTUMN HOUSE
Cover, 1, 5, 6, 7, 9, 12, 21, 23, 24, 25, 26, 28, 30, 32, 33, 35, 36, 44, 45, 49, 50, 54, 57, 58, 60, 61, 62, 65, 67, 69, 71, 72, 74, 75, 76, 81, 89, 90, 93, 95, 97, 99, 100, 105, 107, 113, 115, 119, 121, 122, 135, 138, 141, 149, 150, 158, 161, 164, 167, 169, 173, 174, 176 (inset), 177, 178, 179, 180, 183.

Special thanks to Stanborough School, Watford, England for the photographic use of their premises and for the patience and co-operation of the staff.

Thanks also to Anita, Collette, Grace, Cathy, Natasha, Olivia, Page, Tanya, Trina, Isabel, Bjorn, Enoch, Foday, Jeremy, Jonathan, Lade, Oliver, Raymond and Tunde.

LUDWIG WERNER BINEMANN
5 (left), 11, 13, 22, 42, 51, 83, 85, 112, 132, 181.

SCIENCE PHOTO LIBRARY
Bill Longcore 38, Richard G. Rawlins/Custom Medical Stock 39 (left), BSIP/VEM 39 (top), BSIP/ROUX 137, National Institute of Health 145, Custom Medical Stock 156.

CLIFFORD SHIRLEY
78, 171.